SHE DID THAT!

SHE DID THAT!

STORIES OF EMPOWERMENT

TIA HUDSON

NEW DEGREE PRESS
COPYRIGHT © 2020 TIA HUDSON
All rights reserved.

SHE DID THAT!
Stories of Empowerment

ISBN	978-1-64137-990-8	*Paperback*
	978-1-64137-887-1	*Kindle Ebook*
	978-1-64137-888-8	*Ebook*

CONTENTS

CHAPTER 1.	DEDICATIONS/ACKNOWLEDGEMENTS	7
CHAPTER 2.	INTRODUCTION	11
CHAPTER 3.	AMBITION	17
CHAPTER 4.	THE IMPORTANCE OF PHILANTHROPY	29
CHAPTER 5.	USE YOUR PLATFORM FOR THE BETTER	39
CHAPTER 6.	ADOPT A POSITIVE ATTITUDE	51
CHAPTER 7.	SELF-CONFIDENCE	59
CHAPTER 8.	FIND THE FUN IN EVERYTHING YOU DO	67
CHAPTER 9.	STRENGTH AND POWER IN NUMBERS	77
CHAPTER 10.	GET OUT OF YOUR COMFORT ZONE!	87
CHAPTER 11.	SELF-LOVE	95
CHAPTER 12.	MAKE YOUR MARK IN HISTORY	105
CHAPTER 13.	STEP, EMPOWER, AND UPLIFT EACH OTHER	113
CHAPTER 14.	FIND YOUR PASSION	121
CHAPTER 15.	ENDING MESSAGE	129
CHAPTER 16.	APPENDIX	131

DEDICATIONS/ ACKNOWLEDGEMENTS

To Eric and Natalie:

You both have been the most supportive outlets to me throughout this entire process!

Professor Koester sought me out and believed in me from a very early stage, which I found to be such a compliment. I had absolutely no idea what I was doing when the program started. I had no idea what topic I wanted to focus on, let alone how to write an entire manuscript. But at every hurdle, Eric (without even realising it) helped me see it was nothing I couldn't handle, and I needed that reassurance more than we were both aware of.

Thank you Professor, for believing in me.

Natalie has always been there to provide nothing but positive energy, which was nothing but uplifting to me. After our weekly calls, I was always left with a smile on my face and ready to work and achieve everything I was dreaming of! In the darkest hours, Natalie was always there to be a ray of sunshine to me, which I needed throughout this process.

Thank you Natalie, for uplifting me.

Working with you both has been nothing short of a pleasure.

I want to thank Cameron for also being one of the most prominent forces of stability and hope throughout this entire process. Every time I came up with 100 reasons why I couldn't do this, you gave me 100 reasons why I could.

The world would be a magical place if more people were like you. Thank you for always being there.

I would also like to thank my oldest and greatest friend, who goes by the name of God. The ever-present strength that always provides me with the confidence that I need.

This Book is Dedicated to:

My Daddy:

My twin soul, my everything.

I hope this book brings a smile to your face, wherever you are.

My Mum:

The strongest woman I know, and my first example of a Boss in the flesh.

Thank you for always being my rock and my number one support system.

For My Grandmothers, and my Aunties:

I feel so blessed to have been surrounded by nothing but strong, powerful, and incredible women in my family.

You are all amazing, and I love you wholeheartedly.

Thank you all for paving the way for me.

This book is also dedicated to everyone who was able to pre-order a copy of this book!

Amy Springett, Chloe Hoogwerf, Isobel Gomez, Michelle Williams, Kathy Hoogwerf, Grace Hasson, Sandra Williams, Victoria Lochead, Eric Koester, Cameron Hoogwerf, Ruby Ladley, Tiffany Alves, Martha Gisaw, Patsy Hudson, Erica Hudson, Rebecca Kingsley, Judy Williams, Cindy M. Dennis, Helena Phillips, Lizzie Musa, Augustina Collins, and Rachel Hunt-Bailey.

INTRODUCTION

―

"SHE BELIEVED SHE COULD, SO SHE DID."

This is a phrase that will go on to shift the mindsets of many and create a new generation of confident and powerful women. Clearly, this ideology has the potential to reveal the strategy to empower millions of young women across the planet and will encourage them to live up to their highest potential, in the best way.

When an eleven-year-old Meghan Markle protested against a Procter & Gamble television commercial that she found to be sexist, she could not have possibly predicted the way that her dominant feminist ideals and beliefs would go on to shape her career and inspire millions of women worldwide (including myself).[1] That single act of protest set off a series of possibilities. It gave birth to Meghan The Advocate—the woman who still to this day continues to fight gender inequalities and empower women from all walks of life. Fortunately for

---

1   Andrew Morton, *Meghan: A Hollywood Princess* (London: Michael O'Hara Books Ltd, 2018), 40–1, accessed July 5, 2020.

us, she is incredible at what she does, hence why so many people are empowered by her.[2]

That sheer dedication to supporting female advancement is one of the main reasons why you are holding a copy of this book in your hands. The now Duchess of Sussex along with many other women in our society are continuing to fight against the unfair stereotypes that are unfortunately associated with the female gender. She was calling on all of us to use our voices—and it's powerful. So, I decided to investigate and live by her unique message. Too often we hear, "Be one of the boys to break the glass ceiling," but Meghan offered a different voice. Over the past year, I've wanted to study some of today's most inspiring women, realising that they are all doing something very different and that we can all learn from their ways.

Just as Duchess Meghan states: "If things are wrong and there is a lack of justice, and there is an inequality, then someone needs to say something."[3] Today, we are living in a very fragile society, in which we risk offending someone by voicing our opinions and views on a subject. This book is a source of encouragement for you all to discover the sheer value of your voice and recognise that speaking up about your passions and viewpoints can take you very far in life. As scary as it might be to conceptualise, there is always something oddly thrilling about overcoming your biggest fears.

---

2   Ibid.
3   *The Queen's Commonwealth Trust,* "The Queen's Commonwealth Trust International Women's Day Panel-Full Discussion." March 8, 2019, video, 20:10.

I've always liked to adopt a "march of progress" view in regard to the advancement of women. Undeniably, we have all come a remarkably long way. However, I fear that we have come to an unfortunate bump in the road and that the entire issue of female empowerment has been put on somewhat of a "back-burner." Several setbacks go hand in hand with being a woman in the twenty-first century, both at home and in the workplace.

Speaking up brings clarity. Clarity brings unity. Unity almost always results in happiness. This is another fundamental part of the book that I would like to be stressed. We are living in a time when happiness and positivity have become less of a priority in the lives of many, which is very hard to comprehend. In my view, happiness and positivity are an absolute necessity. It makes me sad to know that these two important emotions are frequently overlooked or sacrificed. I hope this book can help you prioritise your happiness and well-being. If anything, I pray that it will become your ray of sunshine on a dark day and serve as a physical reminder to put effort into making yourself and everyone around you smile more often.

Within the United Kingdom, the gender pay gap among full-time employees stands at 8.9 percent.[4] Additionally, the world average among top female executives is a mere 8 percent (9 percent in the United Kingdom and 5 percent in the United States).[5] Eight percent might not seem like a significant amount of money, but nonetheless it results in

---

[4] Roger Smith, "Gender Pay Gap in the UK: 2019," Office for National Statistics, October 29, 2019.

[5] Ibid.

men receiving more money than women. Possible reasons for this could stem from the general societal consensus of women still being expected to take ownership of all domestic and child-rearing roles. This combined with the current leader of the free world holding a view on women that is very questionable simply goes to show that there doesn't seem to be a lot of opportunities for women to thrive in the ways they are capable of, despite the time period we are living in. Not to mention, according to the *Los Angeles Times,* 13 percent of people in the USA now describe themselves as "not happy" in comparison to 8 percent in 1990.[6] Consumerism has also been identified as the biggest suppressant of happiness. This gives a lot of food for thought.

These facts and statistics can easily be seen as alarming and appear to be projecting the message of equating success, happiness, and breaking the glass ceiling with being "one of the boys." I think that it's appropriate to disassociate with this outdated paradigm, and instead focus on proving the stats wrong. Now is the time to show the world that being "one of the girls," becoming the epitome of positivity, and being provided with the same opportunities as our male counterparts can have an equal, if not more powerful, purpose for the future.

Many factors went into the reason why I felt the need to write this book. First, I felt that there was no better time to support the ongoing cause of female advancement given the climate we are living in and the surge of positivity that

---

[6] Christopher Ingraham, "Americans Are Becoming Less Happy, and There's Research to Prove It," Los Angeles Times, March 23, 2019.

has been associated with these movement as of late. We are living in an age where historical movements such as "Me Too" and "Time's Up" have emphasised a need for all women to form a united front to support one another in addition to influential celebrities openly identifying as feminists. I felt so empowered by all of this positivity that I felt compelled to do my best to contribute in any way possible and make my mark on the world through this book. I have learned the value of using your voice to advocate for issues that are close to your heart, therefore, I felt that it only made sense to make a stand through this medium.

However, I also felt an even stronger need to compose this as I have seen that possessing the power to inspire those around you is a gift more rewarding than many things in life. This book came into the flesh because I felt inspired by every woman that has been included in these pages. They have uplifted the lives of many and brought a large degree of much-needed positivity into the world. They have reassured the unsure, provided guidance for the lost, and instilled belief in the insecure. So now I want to do the same for you. To be fair, I will bring my fair share of positivity into the world and do the same thing for you, as these incredible women have done for me.

No matter what stage you may be in within your life whether it's high school, university, the workforce, or motherhood, it is not uncommon to feel uncertain about what direction to go in, or question who you are as a person. I want this book to be a way for all women to feel empowered about themselves and their lives along with being a source of encouragement for you to go into the world and live up to your best potential, with the "She Did That" mentality eventually becoming second nature to all of you.

I was twenty years old when this fantastic journey began. By the time this book is published, I will have graduated and headed into the next phase of my life. I feel so blessed to have been able to share my thoughts and words in a project that I will never forget. I hope this book brings everyone who reads it nothing but sheer happiness. Thank you for picking this book up, and I hope you enjoy it!

CHAPTER 1

AMBITION

Quote "Oh, it's delightful to have ambitions. I'm so glad I have such a lot.
And there never seems to be an end to them, that's the best of it. Just as soon as you attain to one ambition, you see another glittering higher up still.
It does make life so interesting."

—L.M. MONTGOMERY, ANNE OF GREEN GABLES

SPOTLIGHT ON: VALERIE AMOS

We've all heard the James Brown song "It's a Man's Man's Man's World."[7] Are we really living in a man's world? Or is the future female? Aren't all men and women equal? Is feminism slowly dying out? Are the advocates that are tirelessly using their voices to make a difference going unheard? Why have women always been seen as an inferior gender? Where

---

7   Songfacts, "It's A Man's Man's Man's World by James Brown – Songfacts," Song Meanings at Songfacts, accessed June 26, 2020.

did this ideology originate from? How much longer will we continue to think like this?

In an age where so much divides us, we are being forced to keep asking these types of questions to continue pushing the needle.

Often, women are viewed as delicate, defenceless damsels in distress who need to be rescued and/or protected at all costs.8 Institutions such as religion have shown us this view has existed for centuries. Girls are taught this from a young age through the portrayal of many popular Disney princesses. Cinderella, Sleeping Beauty, and Snow White are all waiting to be saved by their courageous Prince Charming. It is very easy to see why the underlying message little girls receive is that it is the job of a man to swoop in and save the world from impending destruction. This has inadvertently led women to aspire to be the second in command and instead fulfil their biological destinies as breeders, not leaders.[9]

Thankfully, times have evolved slightly, and women have the freedom to have children along with a professional career. Yet, oftentimes, this ancient ideology still lingers in the background. The thought of electing a female president of the United States is alarming and unthinkable to some people, and 34 percent of the members of The House of Commons

---

8   Taylor Hawk, "Passing on Being Passive: Article," Denison University, November 29, 2016.

9   Sylvia Paull, "2000: What Is Today's Most Important Unreported Story?" Edge.org, January 1, 1970.

in the UK are female, which is quite a low number, yet this is the highest it has ever been.[10]

This gives off the message that you have a better chance of achieving excellence in the world if you are male.

However, I believe this message is losing steam. Times are changing. We are moving forward and breaking the simulation with joy! Empowered women from all parts of the world are walking into the new decade with a positive and progressive attitude. The desire to fit into the "male-tinted" view of success no longer exists, as we are now recognising that we can forge a new path for ourselves.

Trying to "think like a man" is overrated. We are "putting on our big girl pants" and creating a legacy for the women that will follow us. It is our time now. Think like a boss, act like a boss, and become a boss in the hope that one day, others will look back on all of your success and say, "She Did That!"

These types of strong and unstoppable females are unapologetically ambitious.

* * *

When thinking of women that fit into this category, I immediately thought of the females that work for the United Nations (UN). I have always held a deep admiration for these

---

10   Christopher Watson, Elise Uberoi, and Esme Kirk-Wade, "Women in Parliament and Government," *House of Commons Library*, May 31, 2020.

fearless women. For over seventy-five years, they have been providing an influence of peace and security throughout the world and upholding human rights and international law.[11] Their relevance and importance have never been lost on me.

It was through the UN that I came across the works of Baroness Valerie Amos, an incredible woman who has broken barriers of stigmatised racism and sexism while making a distinct mark for herself in history. She is proof that having high ambitions and working hard always pays off in the long run. She never let the odds against her limit her ability to dream big and aspire to greatness. She is a true icon.

Valerie Amos was born in Guyana and came to the UK at the age of nine.[12] She has described her experience of first entering England as "funny," perhaps more in the peculiar sense. Entering the UK in the 1960s when racism was at its height was a struggle to the baroness and her family. She spoke of her childhood experiences in an interesting interview I came across on SOAS Radio.[13]

She told the interviewer of a time when her parents were hoping to purchase a house in Southeast London but were met

---

[11] IISD's SDG Knowledge Hub, "Event: Commemoration of the 75th Anniversary of the UN: SDG Knowledge Hub: IISD," SDG Knowledge Hub, 2020, accessed July 5, 2020.

[12] The Editors of Encyclopaedia Britannica, "Valerie Ann Amos, Baroness Amos of Brondesbury," Encyclopædia Britannica (Encyclopædia Britannica, inc., March 9, 2020.

[13] "CISD Presents: New Beings and Women's Empowerment Group in Discussion with Baroness Valerie Amos," SOAS Radio, October 31, 2018.

with disapproval from people in the area who had started a petition to ensure that their desired purchase would not go ahead.[14] (Very reminiscent of the plotline for the play "*A Raisin in the Sun,*" for anyone who is a fan of Lorraine Hansberry.) Fortunately, the Amos family had "good neighbours" who ensured that no one signed the petition.[15]

These setbacks never deterred Baroness Amos from the vision she had for her career. She understood the obstacles ahead of her, but she had faith in her intelligence. She never let her high ambitions for herself fade, and this strategy has worked in her favour. In 2011, *Forbes* magazine listed her as one of the "Ten Most Powerful Women in the United Nations."[16]

The list of Valerie Amos' achievements is endless. She is the first black woman to sit in the cabinet for the United Kingdom, the first black woman to be a director of a university in the United Kingdom (SOAS), and the first black woman to be the head of an Oxford College.[17] She worked as Under-Secretary-General for Humanitarian Affairs and as an Emergency Relief Coordinator.[18] In 2012, she visited Syria to help those

---

14 Ibid.

15 Ibid.

16 Avril David, "The 10 Most Powerful Women at the United Nations," *Forbes,* September 2, 2011.

17 "Baroness Valerie Amos Appointed as Master of University College," University of Oxford, 2019, accessed July 5, 2020.

18 "Under-Secretary-General for Humanitarian Affairs and Emergency Relief Coordinator, Valerie Amos Statement on Yemen – Yemen," ReliefWeb, accessed July 5, 2020.

affected by the uprising.[19] As the interviewer continued to ask her about the most significant achievement in her career, she understandably admitted that it was "hard to point to just one thing, as [she's] done a range of different jobs and [she has] learned from every single one of those experiences."[20]

In regard to her success as a woman of colour in Britain, she has bypassed all the existing negative statistics and excelled. In the UK, 3 percent of our most powerful and influential people are from black and minority ethnic groups, according to *The Guardian* newspaper.[21]

Despite the fact that many people tried to put her down by saying Amos achieved all these things because of quotas intended to increase the percentage of minorities in elected office, the baroness is strong in her assertion that her success is due to her ambition and hard work.

"Many people in my career . . . basically looked me in the face and said that I've only got there because it was the right place, the right time, and because of a quota or because of a target. I know because I have the confidence to know that I have worked extremely hard, that I don't feel that I have ever,

---

19 Matthew Weaver, "Valerie Amos and Kofi Annan to Visit Syria – Monday 5 March 2012," The Guardian (Guardian News and Media, March 5, 2012).
20 "CISD Presents: New Beings and Women's Empowerment Group in Discussion with Baroness Valerie Amos," SOAS Radio, October 31, 2018.
21 Pamela Duncan and Josh Holder, "Revealed: Britain's Most Powerful Elite Is 97% White," *The Guardian*, September 24, 2017.

ever got a job, on the basis of a quota, or a target," Baroness Amos said.[22]

An ambitious woman is usually perceived as someone who "has it all together."[23] They are usually associated with the "go-getter" part of the population who are truly passionate about what they do. As a result, they are often treated with a high level of respect and importance by those who surround them. So, in short, your ambition plays a large role in shaping how you are viewed.

A poll of three thousand women carried out by *Business Insider* found that most women identified as ambitious when it comes to their careers, but only about one-third were comfortable using the word "ambitious" to describe themselves.[24] A psychological standpoint suggested that this was due to the negative labelling associated with the term. They believe that women who define themselves as ambitious are often seen as aggressive. Denise Pickett, the president of the global services group at American Express, believes that it crucial for a woman to discard the stigma attached to the word "ambition" and encourages all women to embrace it

---

22   Pamela Duncan and Josh Holder, *"Revealed: Britain's Most Powerful Elite Is 97% White,"* The Guardian (Guardian News and Media, September 24, 2017).

23   Marie-Claire Chappet, "Seriously, Why Are We Still Asking If Women Can 'Have It All?'" Glamour (Glamour UK, March 20, 2019).

24   Marguerite Ward, "Women Are Afraid to Call Themselves "Ambitious" at Work and It's Seriously Hurting Their Careers," Business Insider (Business Insider, March 8, 2020).

as a lifestyle choice.[25] She stated that by openly articulating our ambitions along with the obstacles and difficulties we are likely to embrace while chasing them, we give ourselves a better chance of finding the right advocates to help alleviate the struggles and difficulties that are stopping us from achieving greatness. This message is fundamental. Never allow your ambition to fade.[26]

I came across an interview Ms. Amos had done with *The Huffington Post,* and it was here she stated that she credits a great deal of her success to taking risks in her career and adopting a positive attitude.[27]

She instructed anyone that was reading the article to "take the risk, have a bit of fun and learn along the way."[28] She believes that life is all about learning and that it is important to focus on what you can learn from the things that did not go the way you planned. She wholeheartedly equates taking risks to achieving success and says that you cannot get a sense of what you are capable of achieving if you are risk-averse.[29]

---

25 "'Chasing Skills, Not Levels,' a Recipe for Women's Success in the Corporate World," The Globe and Mail, September 7, 2019.
26 Marguerite Ward, "Women Are Afraid to Call Themselves 'Ambitious' at Work and It's Seriously Hurting Their Careers," *Business Insider,* March 8, 2020.
27 Natasha Hinde, *"The First Black Woman in British Cabinet, Baroness Valerie Amos, Shares Her Secrets for Success"* The Huffington Post (The Huffington Post, April 22, 2016).
28 Ibid.
29 Ibid.

So, I encourage all of you to follow in the steps of Baroness Amos. Always think of the wonders of what could happen if you put yourself out there and take a chance on yourself. After doing all of this research, one thing I have learned from Amos is to just go for it. Through this mentality, Amos has managed to change the course of history for herself and women of colour in Britain. She is living proof that it is possible to break the simulation and achieve your wildest dreams regardless of your ethnicity or socioeconomic background, and she has shown us all how to do so.

Ms. Amos' ambition has taught me a magnitude of unspoken lessons and allowed me to see the value of ambition clearer than ever. Her story showed me that fear is capable of coming in many forms, including doubt, lack of confidence, and lack of self-belief; the list is endless. But she represents something more obvious here. She has shown us that ambition is stronger than any form of fear combined. The burning desire you have to achieve your dreams can be pushed forward with the power of ambition.

I lacked ambition when I was younger, but I am proud to say that I have more ambition in me now than I ever have before. In my teenage years, I would constantly doubt myself and my abilities, especially when it came to school and exams. Before I continue, I apologize if this sounds cringy. I know that in today's society, everyone seems to have a story about when they were doubted in school in some way. However, it is important to take note of the one quality that all of those school-doubting success stories have in common . . . ambition. That sheer drive to "prove the nay-sayers wrong" no matter what has pulled a countless amount of people through their education and careers, myself included. I remember having a strong desire to prove my academic abilities to myself and others during the years I took my General Certificate of Secondary Education (GCSE) exams. I was sixteen years old, and I remember feeling hurt and disappointed when I saw what my teachers had predicted me to achieve. I knew I was capable of doing better and made it my mission to prove that to everyone. My ambition to show my academic worth pulled me through and worked very well in my favour, as I ended up scoring significantly higher than what I was predicted to. It goes to show that ambition will rarely fail you.

Many women are cautious about being labelled as "too ambitious" as it can come across as bragging, along with opening you up to unwanted judgment and hearing comments such as, "Who does she think she is?" Here is the good news: Those opinions are totally irrelevant and meaningless. If you are passionate about something, chase it. Grab it with both hands and don't let go of it. Ambition is healthy! Don't let anyone else tell you otherwise.

* * *

Luckily, many ways of raising your ambition levels exist. Start by writing out your goals and outline exactly what it is you want to achieve. Having a clear picture will make the process a lot easier. Once you have done this, simply go after your desire. Apologies if you were expecting a long and detailed method! That's all there is. Other than being on the lookout for what inspires you, whether it be a person, a story, a piece of art, or an opinion, having ambition is, fortunately, the easy part of achieving your dreams!

Including Ms. Amos in this book has been a delightful pleasure. After finalising her as a feature, I spent ages trying to decipher what category to place her story under, since she is a woman of many talents and emits loads of important life lessons simultaneously. I feel that ambition is a notion that complements her career well. I hope you have enjoyed reading about the baroness as much as I have.

A woman who can disrupt historical standards will always remain as an undeniable Boss and will always leave people in admiration while mentally stating, "She Did That!"

Action Items of the Chapter

- FIND WHAT INSPIRES YOU.
- PIN-POINT WHAT YOU ARE GOING TO DO WITH YOUR
- NEWFOUND AMBITION.
- GO AND DO IT!

CHAPTER 2

THE IMPORTANCE OF PHILANTHROPY

"Love is not patronising and charity is not about pity, it's about love.
Charity and love are the same.
With charity you give love, so don't give money but reach out your hand instead."

—MOTHER TERESA

SPOTLIGHT ON: OPRAH WINFREY
Imagine this:

It's the year 3005. A worldwide law has just been passed that states that each resident of planet Earth who earns an income must donate 50 percent of their earnings to a charity of their choice. Would you say this law is reasonable? Is that figure too high? Should we be required to donate to charities?

A lot of questions, and so much to consider.

* * *

Within today's current climate, nearly half of the world's population can be categorised as "poor."[30] Economic advances around the world mean that while fewer people live in extreme poverty, almost half of the world's population—3.4 billion people—still struggle to meet basic needs, according to the World Bank.[31] As Beyoncé has previously stated in her music, a large majority of people work "nine to five to stay alive."[32] In times like this, the thought of giving back to charities and individuals less fortunate than ourselves is sadly one of the last things occupying our minds. However, it is undeniable that simply looking at these scary facts and figures should be enough of a wake-up call to rally together. UNICEF reports that approximately twenty-two thousand children die each day due to poverty.[33] Therefore, giving a helping hand to the less fortunate, if we are in the position to do so, can go a very long way in the grand scheme of things.

Philanthropy is a concept that has become foreign to the younger citizens of our world. I feel that a big difference can be made if our current generation became more focused on others. Of course, a lot of children and young adolescents are not able to give large amounts of money, but every donation counts, regardless of how big or small it is. Just a simple hour

---

30 "Poverty Overview," The World Bank, 2020, accessed July 5, 2020.

31 Elizabeth Howton, "Nearly Half the World Lives on Less than $5.50 a Day," *World Bank*, 2018.

32 "Beyoncé – Haunted," Genius, December 13, 2013.

33 Christian Moer, "Child Mortality Rate Drops by a Third Since 1990," *UNICEF*, September 16, 2010.

of your time can make a significant difference in someone's life. It all starts with the first step, and the woman I am about to introduce proves my theory to be accurate.

Oprah Gail Winfrey is a name that has become known worldwide. She is someone who has worked very hard and has achieved an abundance of success. Her unique ability to connect with her audience and establish an emotional bond with them by opening up about some of the traumatic events she has lived through is perhaps what allows the public to understand the reasons behind her enthusiasm for philanthropy. At the time, I'm sure those who knew this woman would be shocked to discover that she would go on to become the richest African American of the twentieth century.[34] Years ago, she was once demoted from Baltimore's WJZ-TV for being too emotionally invested in the stories she was covering and deemed "unfit for television news."[35] Now, she has a net worth of $2.7 billion as of 2019, which takes her to the top of the list of female icons across the world.[36]

Philanthropic principles have always been at the centre of Oprah's core values. Being heavily immersed in spirituality and the karmic laws of the universe which dictate that you create your own path in life based on the amount of good or

---

34   Stephanie Ogbogu, "Oprah Is the Richest Black Woman in the World," AfroTech, 2020, accessed July 5, 2020.

35   Rachel Gillett, "How Walt Disney, Oprah Winfrey, and 19 Other Successful People Rebounded After Getting Fired," Inc.com (Inc., October 7, 2015).

36   6th July 2020 by Spear's, "Oprah Winfrey's Net Worth," Spear's Magazine, January 25, 2018.

bad you offer the world.[37] Oprah has always advocated that your views, beliefs, and attitudes are a reflection on your life circumstances.[38] Whatever you put out into the universe will return to you at some point, hence why she places such importance on giving back to charity as a method of counting all of her blessings.

When I see the amount of work, time, money, and effort Oprah has put into her charity work, I feel so inspired to also create a platform as life changing and positive as hers. I feel so proud and blessed to have lived in the same time as her. She has established charity foundations such as "Oprah's Angel Network," which has raised over $80 million for non-profit organisations across the globe, and established her own school in South Africa, which is called "The Oprah Winfrey Leadership Academy for Girls."[39] Not to mention her own foundation, which is living proof of her "hands-on" approach toward her philanthropy projects, which usually involves seeing herself as equal to the people that she is helping. This has proven to be the best way for Oprah to achieve success. Through her dedication and actions, Oprah is teaching a magnitude of young girls from all different walks of life about the importance of counting your blessings through philanthropy and showing how it emphasises unity in our community. You can never feel guilty for the blessings you've

---

37   Katherine Hurst, "Cause and Effect Meaning: The 12 Laws of Karma List," The Law Of Attraction, October 9, 2019, accessed July 5, 2020.

38   Rebecca Achilles, "Oprah Winfrey Credits Her Success to This One Thing We All Have," Medium (Thoughts and Ideas, December 6, 2018).

39   Candid, "Oprah Winfrey's Angel Network to Dissolve," Philanthropy News Digest (PND), June 1, 2010.

been gifted if you remember to lend a helping hand to an individual who is less fortunate than you. It makes the world a better place in every way you look at it.

The formation of "The Oprah Winfrey Leadership Academy for Girls" is one of my favourite Oprah projects. It was an idea that originated from the simple factors of belief, desire, and determination.[40] Winfrey believed that many girls in South Africa who were living in poverty possessed the power to hold central leadership roles if they were given the right tools and an environment in which to excel.[41] Not only did she believe wholeheartedly in these girls, but she was also determined to manifest her vision. Twelve years later and the school is still standing as a huge success, much to Oprah's joy.

According to Oprah, the inspiration to build a school came to her while visiting the house of Nelson Mandela in 2002.[42] They both discussed the project and agreed on the idea of education being a useful tool to help end poverty in South Africa.[43] When the academy launched five years later, Oprah's heart was filled with joy. This tripled when she witnessed the graduations of seventy-two students within the program.

"All of those young ladies were accepted into universities and colleges in and around South Africa as well as in the United States. Our alumnae are now graduating from college and

---

40 Kathy Crockett, "Oprah Winfrey's Leadership Academy for Girls," The MY HERO Project, 2020, accessed July 5, 2020.

41 "Graduating Class of 2019," OWLAG, accessed July 5, 2020.

42 Ibid.

43 Ibid.

university and determining how they are going to make their mark in the world. I could not feel any more honoured and proud of the work they have done to accomplish their goals and achieve their dreams."[44]

What excites Oprah the most is the knowledge that "this is just the beginning."[45] She sees education as a gift that has brought so much positive change to the communities and families of South Africa. The gift of education has the power to transform lives through her perspective. In her words: "When you invest in a young woman you are investing in the future, not only of South Africa but also of the world. So, these young ladies are a symbol and a beacon of light, of what is possible."[46]

Oprah's belief in these young girls and her dedication to providing them with a sufficient amount of education and encouragement paints her as the incredible icon so many people see her as today. To describe her as selfless would be an understatement, and her generosity has no bounds.

Another one my favourite examples of Oprah giving back to the community is none other than the momentous "YOU GET A CAR!" giveaway on her show, a moment that left her viewers in utter shock and remains one of the most unforgettable giveaways of our lifetime.[47] While I was research-

---

44 Ibid.
45 Ibid.
46 Ibid.
47 John Neff, "Oprah's Famous Car Giveaway: 6 Things You Probably Didn't Know," Motor1.com (Motor1.com, April 18, 2019).

ing Oprah's charitable acts, I stumbled across a clip of her reliving that infamous moment, in which she explained her feelings behind it. During this clip, Oprah went on to describe this giveaway as "one of the greatest moments ever." As the clip of the show began to play, it was very heartwarming to see the first eleven selected members of the audience excitedly make their way to the stage, as I knew exactly what they were about to experience.

Once again, Oprah was reaching out to these individuals, who could be considered "less fortunate" than her, and she decided to fulfil their "wildest dreams" by gifting them brand-new cars. This was something each person was "desperately in need of" and was given as a thank you for doing such good work in their teaching profession. Oprah maintained a neutral facial expression throughout and was careful not to spoil the surprise she was about to unload on the rest of the audience, which made it that much more special. Her method of keeping the audience intrigued by telling them that she had "one car left," which a lucky member of the audience would get to go home with, was mesmerising.

And then it happened.

The moment of euphoria, where everyone in the studio, including Oprah herself, began to jump and scream in excitement as everyone in the audience received a key to their brand-new car. This action filled each audience member's heart with joy.

When reflecting on this moment, Oprah went on to state, "People were screaming so loudly that I thought that they didn't understand or wouldn't understand what had just happened. And what is just thrilling about that moment is that you can see the wave of understanding hitting each person. Because at first, at one moment, everyone is holding up the keys, and then a black woman stands up and mouths, 'Are you kidding me?!'[48] And then she looks over at her friend and sees that she has one and is like what?! You have one? But I have one too!"[49] Judging by the expression on Oprah's elated face, you could see that bringing others joy simultaneously brings her joy as well. The art of giving back has been a key component of her personal happiness, along with thousands of others.

* * *

A story of philanthropy that I have always found remarkable is from Rhonda Byrne, who is best known for being the author of a famous book called *The Secret*. This story contains a strong message about the power of giving back and includes the same principles of philanthropy that Oprah is preaching.

When she was in the middle of producing the movie version of *The Secret,* Rhonda admitted she was finding it very hard to make ends meet.[50] She would get calls every day concerning something that needed to be paid for, she was millions of dollars over budget for the film, and had no idea

---

48 Ibid.
49 Ibid.
50 "Rhonda Byrne Biography: The Secret – Official Website," The Official Website of The Secret, accessed July 3, 2020.

how she was going to pay her staff.[51] What makes this story remarkable is the decision Rhonda made regarding how she was going to cope with all the stress. Instead of the typical money management skills and budget strategies you would typically expect someone to attempt, Rhonda went to the nearest cash machine/ATM, withdrew "several hundred dollars," and started giving out her money to people in the street.[52] She was in the eye of the storm but still felt a duty to help and support the people around her. She knew she needed that money for bills and groceries, but also understood there were some individuals who needed the money more urgently than she did. Rhonda managed to put her faith in the "what you give out, you will receive back twice as strong" principle and acted selflessly with money she had worked hard for. Throughout this whole exchange, she was shocked to find how good it felt to give the money away and see the glow in an individual's face as she handed over the money. She loved being able to see that she had made someone's day better through such a simple act. It showed the mark of a true philanthropist. The principle she was acting upon could not have worked out better for her, as the following Monday after this event, she unexpectedly received $25,000 in her bank account after selling some shares she had forgotten about.[53] It goes to show that the universe will always reward you if you're prepared to extend yourself and be a source of hope and light to the world.

---

51 Ibid.
52 Ibid.
53 Ibid.

* * *

As I previously mentioned, Oprah Winfrey is a woman who has inspired a variety of people across the globe. Whenever the topic of "inspirational women" comes to play, I can guarantee that Oprah's name will cross a large majority of people's minds. It was because of this that I felt it was only necessary to include Oprah in this book, as she continues to effortlessly align herself with my definition of a modern-day Girl-Boss. To me, a true Girl-Boss is an individual who has used her indestructibly strong work ethic to not only bring herself a tremendous amount of success in her own life, but also a woman who selflessly dedicates herself to making the world a better place for us all. Oprah has done this since the beginning of her career, and to this day has not stopped. She is an extraordinary example of a woman who reminds all young girls the importance of seeing how fortunate we all are along with always seeing the glass half full in every situation we encounter. An icon, an entrepreneur, and an inspiration. It is hard to not look back at everything she has achieved in her career and think, "She Did That!"

Below are a handful of a few charities that Oprah has frequently donated to. Feel free to check them out and join in on the philanthropy quest.

- Free the Children
- Elevate Hope Foundation
- Peace Over Violence
- UNICEF
- Born This Way Foundation

CHAPTER 3

USE YOUR PLATFORM FOR THE BETTER

"Stand for what is right. Even if it means standing alone."

—SUZY KASSEEM

SPOTLIGHT ON: AMERICA FERRERA
Quick food for thought: What do you stand for in life?

* * *

We all have a platform in our lives, whether it's big or small. A very wise man once stated that "All the world's a stage, and all the men and women are merely players."[54] A big concept

---

54 Posted by Denis McLaughlin, "Leaders: All the World's a Stage. And All the Men and Women Are Merely Players," accessed July 5, 2020.

to consider is how we should be using our personal platforms. Some of us use it to influence, while others use it to entertain. Some use it to advocate, while others choose to send a deeper message. One of the many pleasures in our lives is that we get to control what we use our platforms for, and it can often end up defining us as people. Many admirable people in this world dedicate themselves solely to making the planet a happier place to inhabit. A woman who immediately springs to my mind when talking of such people is none other than America Ferrera.

I chose to feature Ferrera in this book for a multitude of reasons. The first reason is because she was recommended to me by my editor, Melody. At this point, I had known very little about her. Other than the fact that she starred in the world-famous TV series *Ugly Betty,* I knew nothing about her. However, after doing some research on her career and watching a mesmerizing TED Talk of hers, I felt not only compelled but obligated to feature this incredible woman. America has not only managed to establish an incredible career as an actress, but she has solidified herself as a strong activist for female rights and immigration justice.[55] She is an inspiration to the world, and I am very impressed with everything she has achieved. I hope after reading this, she makes it onto your personal list of female icons.

After watching America speak so passionately on the pressing issues of racism and immigration, I began to do my research

---

55   Ann Marie Deer Owens, "America Ferrera to Discuss 'Life Between Cultures' at Chancellor's Lecture," Vanderbilt University (Vanderbilt University, February 3, 1970).

and try to see some examples of what she was talking about. I was not very aware of the immigration issues that occur in the US; however, I am now very aware of the current state of US immigration legislation and the scary consequences it can have for many individuals. Currently, the United States has a larger immigration population than any other country in the world. More than forty million people living in the US were born in another country, accounting for about one-fifth of the world's immigrants in 2017.[56] Seven hundred fifty thousand of them are part of the younger generation, according to Ferrera.[57] US border agents process only a handful of the asylum requests a day, which has unfortunately led to serious overcrowding in shelters at the border, along with a huge backlog of applications.[58] After looking at figures like this, it is clear to me why Ferrera feels such a strong need to lend her name and likeness to fight and change these situations. Thankfully, she is very good at what she does. It brings me such pride to say that in a period of such dark times, Ferrera uses her platform to offer everyone hope. Constantly speaking and bringing awareness to the injustices that are occurring and encouraging everyone to fix the situation is the precise way that she uses her personal stage for the better.

America Ferrera is the perfect example of an empowered woman who uses her platform to bring awareness to causes

---

[56] Jynnah Radford, "Key Findings about US Immigrants," Pew Research Center (Pew Research Center, June 17, 2019).

[57] Mathew Rodriguez, "America Ferrera's Women's March Address Stood in Solidarity with Young Undocumented Immigrants," *Mic*, January 21, 2017).

[58] Ibid.

that have significant meaning to her. Not only is she a notable advocate for immigration injustice, but she has also lent her voice to issues of female injustices in our society. She has spoken very openly about the struggles she has faced as a Latin American woman in the entertainment industry, and she is trying to display her experiences as a catalyst to enforce change. One of the most famous examples of Ferrera speaking out on her experiences is a speech she did in a TED Talk.[59] She made this speech with the hope that no other woman in Hollywood (regardless of their ethnicity) would have to go through the same thing.

In her speech, Ferrera spoke about her dream to become an actress, mostly because she had never seen anyone that looked like her on television.[60] She made it her mission to chase her dream, despite those around her stating, "People like [you] don't make it in Hollywood."[61] Her American identity is what encouraged her to ignore the negativity and go after her desire. She boldly stated that it didn't matter if she was the daughter of two immigrants from Honduras, "I didn't need my dream to be easy, I just needed it to be possible."[62] Ferrera's climb to the top was filled with difficulty in the beginning, which was mostly due to the offensive stereotypical acting roles that were available to her.[63] The only roles she was provided with included

---

59 America Ferrera, "My Identity Is a Superpower—Not an Obstacle," *TED*, 2019.
60 Ibid
61 Ibid.
62 Ibid.
63 Ibid.

"sassy shoplifter," "gangbanger's girlfriend," and "pregnant chola number two"[64] (chola is a Spanish term for a woman associated with gang culture). She finally decided that enough was enough and complained to her manager about the limiting types of roles that she was getting and informed him that she instead would like to play more complex characters that were more central to the plotline, rather than background characters. His response was beyond disappointing, but it motivated Ferrera to work even harder. He walked away from the conversation saying:

"Someone has to tell that girl that she has unrealistic expectations."[65] This response got him fired. Unfortunately, this was not the last time Ferrera would receive disappointing and infuriating comments from prominent figures within the acting world. She was turned away by countless jobs on the basis of them not wishing to cast the role diversely. It gave the impression that her identity was a personal obstacle, to which she responded with

"Come at me obstacle! I am an American! MY NAME IS AMERICA!"[66]

Watching this TED Talk made me feel empowered. I felt so proud to see America advocating for an issue that has been the cause of many divisions within the world we all live in. Her method of being so blunt and open about the harsh experiences that she has faced gives an infinite amount of power

---

64 Ibid.
65 Ibid.
66 Ibid.

to make her speeches more magnetic. Many women in the world can relate to her experiences, which is perhaps her motivation for bringing justice to all of these situations and circumstances. What I admired about this speech the most was the fact that she was using her platform to teach young girls to be proud of their nationalities, as it is a fundamental part of who they are. Her speech was a way of leading by example and displaying the uniqueness of being different and standing out from what the stereotypical norm is considered to be. We need more women like America Ferrera in this world—women who encourage others to tackle adversity head-on and to not be afraid of it.

In true empowered-woman fashion, America spends a great deal of her time trying to bring awareness to the issues she feels need more attention in the mainstream media. An issue she has been dedicated to improving for the last couple of years is Women's Rights.[67] A speech she delivered during the 2017 Women's March remains as one of the most impactful speeches of her career. America decided to speak out against President Trump's controversial opinions on women's issues and made an impact on millions of minds across the United States.[68] The level of passion and urgency in America's voice had a distinct unifying effect on her listeners. Her persuasive and declarative style of speaking worked in her favour as

---

67 America Ferrera, "America Ferrera on Activism After the Women's March," Time (Time, March 1, 2018).

68 Tierney McAfee January 21 and Tierney McAfee, "America Ferrera at DC Women's March: 'The President Is Not America. . . . We Are America,'" EW.com, 2017, accessed July 5, 2020.

the audience continued to cheer louder and louder as she continued with her speech:

"We are gathered here and across the country and around the world today to say, 'Mr. Trump, we refuse. We reject the demonization of our Muslim brothers and sisters,' Ferrera said. "We demand an end to the systemic murder and incarceration of our black brothers and sisters. We will not give up our right to safe and legal abortions. We will not ask our LGBTQ families to go backwards. We will not go from being a nation of immigrants, to a nation of ignorance."[69]

Although I am not from the United States, I automatically felt obligated to side with America as she spoke with a phenomenal amount of power and determination. I felt so proud to be a woman when her speech ended. She passionately stated to her audience: *"The President is NOT America. His cabinet is NOT America. Congress is NOT America. We are America, and we are here to stay. We march today for our families and our neighbours, for our future, for the causes we claim and the causes that claim us."*[70] Her use of the collective pronoun "we" was perhaps America's method of connecting with the audience and making them realise that we are all in this fight together. Judging by the reaction of her speech, her method worked. The response from this speech was overwhelmingly positive. Many women were calling on Ferrera to run for office, and people on social media continued to shower her with compliments on her bravery. Having the strength to go up on a stage and display your thoughts and beliefs to an

---

69   Ibid.
70   Ibid.

audience of that magnitude is not an easy task. It shows the depths of courage in America's character, and defines her as a woman who isn't afraid to stand alone for causes that she feels are important.

America is also one of the many celebrities who came together to form the #TimesUp movement.[71] I plan on speaking more about this movement in another chapter, but I just wanted to highlight America's involvement with it here and show her intentions behind the movement:

"It's called #TimesUp and it is a campaign that [was] started by, as you were saying, women in the entertainment industry who have come together to say that we have to leverage our resources, our access, our platform to do better for the conditions of women across all industries in the workplace. And we're saying time's up on the silence, time's up on waiting for things to change, time's up on any behaviour or culture that makes women less safe in the workplace. Women and people of colour, and L.G.B.T.Q community, and disabled people, and anyone else. It stands for all of us."[72]

It seems to me that America is constantly using her platform to advocate for the greater good, and that is why I felt like she was the only woman that could represent the principle I am trying to preach in this book. She is unstoppable and

---

71   Jonathan Borge, "America Ferrera Explains the Importance of the Time's Up Initiative," InStyle, 2018, accessed July 6, 2020.

72   Cara Buckley, "Powerful Hollywood Women Unveil Anti-Harassment Action Plan," The New York Times (The New York Times, January 1, 2018).

refuses to rest until these issues are addressed and dealt with fairly. This is an admirable quality to have.

* * *

America's work has truly set the wheels in motion for me. She represents a very unique form of courage that is hard to ignore. As children, we were always encouraged to keep our opinions to ourselves and just be quiet. To be seen and not heard, if you will. Here, America is offering you the chance to do something different. Taking a stand and speaking openly about subjects that are close to your heart. This book is my first step toward building the foundations of the platform I want to stand on, in addition to abandoning those limiting beliefs that once held me back. I want to generate a source of goodness for the world, and I have no issue using my platform to do so. Say goodbye to those little seeds of doubt that are clouding your ability to be fearless. They are of no use to you anymore. So many more important issues need attention. America has helped me take my first step. Now, I will hopefully help you take yours.

I am writing this paragraph on June 4, 2020. I feel compelled to share how I have decided to use my own platform given the events that are currently occurring today. Not only are we still in the midst of a global pandemic, but we are witnessing the birth of a new generation of change-makers. The murder of George Floyd has sparked a conversation on racial injustice.[73] Being a woman of colour myself, I feel that it is crucial for me to take a stand, and I am choosing to do that by using my platform. Speaking about race within the UK is generally frowned upon. This is an unspoken notion. But seeing the tragedy that has occurred within the US has made me realise the importance of using your voice along with seeing how much you can impact change through doing so. People like America Ferrera prove this theory to be correct. I now feel empowered to use my platform in this way. I want to help create a brighter future for all black people worldwide and help educate anyone who needs any further clarification on the subject. We will be able to make a huge impact if we stick together. I am proud to be using my personal platform to contribute in any way that I can.

I will always have a deep level of admiration for America Ferrera's fierce determination and "go-getter" attitude. She is a fantastic role model for women of all ages and frequently uses her platform to raise awareness for important causes while simultaneously reminding us that we are all part of the female collective. She brings a great degree of positivity to the world and is a living reminder to always fight for the things that are important to you. I hope you all feel encouraged to follow in her footsteps and take a stand for something you feel is important. It doesn't necessarily have to be politics. Just anything you feel has been overlooked unfairly. You are entitled to an opinion, and you have every right to express it, just as America is doing. Featuring her in this book complemented the essence I was hoping to capture, and her

---

73   "George Floyd: 'Pandemic of Racism' Led to His Death, Memorial Told," BBC News (BBC, June 5, 2020).

commitment was something that needed to be praised. A sister to us all, and a Girl-Boss in the flesh.

Action Items for the Chapter:

- What do you want to change in the world?
- What do you want to be known for?
- Chase that desire and dedicate your life to it.

CHAPTER 4

ADOPT A POSITIVE ATTITUDE

"When you are joyful, say yes to life, have fun and project positivity all around you, you become a sun in the centre of every constellation and people want to be near you."

—SHANNON L. ALDER

WOULD YOU CONSIDER YOURSELF TO BE A POSITIVE PERSON?
Do you think it is hard to maintain a positive outlook on life?

* * *

The new age of self-help and self-care has taken a more dominant stance within the last few years. One topic of discussion that stood out to me was the power of positive thinking, and the effects it has had on so many people around the world. It seems like such a simple statement to tell someone to "cheer up" or "don't think like that." We are more likely to carry on maintaining a negative attitude if we hear statements like that, as it is often seen as annoying and much easier said than done. The good news is if you go the right way about it, changing your mindset and training yourself to think more positively has the potential to help you see the world around you in a much brighter light.

To be able to live your life in an empowered fashion, it is important to understand the logistics behind positive thinking, and then apply it to everything you do. Consider optimism to be a gift. To attain it, you must apply all the old sayings you have previously heard your parents and grandparents repeat to you at some point in your life, such as "treat others in the way you would like to be treated," "adopt an attitude of gratitude," or "the glass is half full" to name a few. Positivity is a trait that can be learned, which means it is accessible to everyone. Countless health benefits are associated with positive thinking, which shows its scientific power. Researchers have concluded that adopting a positive attitude can potentially lower your chances of depression and distress, improve your cardiovascular health, build up your resistance against the common cold, and help you cope better with hardship.[74] This provides us all with hope that we can change the world for the better, as long as we put the effort in.

---

74 "How to Stop Negative Self-Talk," Mayo Clinic (Mayo Foundation for Medical Education and Research, January 21, 2020),

* * *

Upon my research for positive thinking, I decided to go straight to the TED Talks website, as they are usually the central hub for every topic you can think of, including positivity. Upon doing this, I saw a speech entitled "The Power of Gratitude and Positive Thinking."[75] The picture next to it showed a young girl, who didn't look any older than the age of fifteen. This startled me as I'd never seen such a young child giving a TED Talk before.

The youngest people I'd ever seen give a speech on TED were usually established adults. So, I decided to click on her talk. Once I had finished watching, I understood completely why it had over one thousand views, and why the comments were so complimentary. This young girl named Dareen told the audience her story of unfairly losing a loved one and how the entire experience almost cast a negative cloud on her for eternity.[76] After this, she went on to insist that while this incident was traumatizing, it caused her to forcefully look for all the positive things in her life to keep afloat.[77] She had decided to "flip the switch" and view this sudden and tragic death as a reason to rejoice and be thankful for the fact that she is still alive and healthy.[78]

---

75 TedXTalks. "The Power of Gratitude and Positive Thinking –Dareen Nasr" TedX AlRabihSchool, July 19, 2019, 9:52 minutes, accessed July 5, 2020.
76 Ibid.
77 Ibid.
78 Ibid.

"Everything bad that has happened to us is only trying to build us up more than we ever could. So without feeling empty from the inside like I did, and I did [truly] feel empty. I hated life for a long while. . . . I am still thankful. Without these obstacles, I wouldn't be the person that I am now. We always look for the missing things and we never value what we have. So let's forget about our painful pasts and accept the present as a gift from God."[79]

I find it amazing that despite her age, Dareen is teaching people of all ages to flip the switch and look at everything from a positive perspective. She was in a situation that could have easily broken her and permanently changed her method of thinking. Instead, she chose to adopt a positive attitude and her choice has paid off well.

* * *

I love to use analogies to prove a point and, with regard to positivity, it is safe to say I have a favourite. When I was in school, one of my teachers came up with an exercise to show us a technique of how our minds work. He instructed us to close our eyes for ten seconds. Once our eyes were opened again, he then told us to count out as many red objects as we could see in the room within thirty seconds. We all felt the same pressure and eagerness to identify as many red objects as possible. When the task was completed, my teacher went on to explain how we wouldn't have identified half of the objects we named if we hadn't been instructed to look out

---

79   Ibid.

for them, which was very true. I thought about that concept a long time after and realized that I could apply it to positivity. If we put our attention on noticing and appreciating the simple things in life that we often take for granted (just as Dareen is instructing us to do), it will open us up to so much more in our day-to-day lives. We would all notice so much positivity in the world if we just put a little more effort in. Small actions like this can make such a big difference in the long run.

Words and communication are both something we all use daily in many different forms. I was very aware of the fact that the way we communicate with ourselves, both mentally and physically, has more of an effect on us than we are aware of. However, an article in *Forbes* magazine enlightened me to the fact that the way we talk about other people can have a similar effect.[80] It told the story of a man named Eugene who was unhappy with his treatment and performance at his place of work but managed to use the method of revising his language to change this.

An interviewer at *Forbes* saw the life of a man named Eugene and wanted to help him try to integrate positive thinking into his work life in an effort to make his experiences better.[81] Eugene was not happy with his work conditions. People who worked closely to him were shocked to hear the way that he

---

80   Peter Himmelman, "The Power of Positive Speech: How Choosing the Right Words Defines Your Reality," Forbes (Forbes Magazine, October 23, 2018).

81   Ibid.

would speak about his job.[82] He would say things such as "This place is insane!" and he would describe his boss, Marcus, as an "assh*le" frequently, also often accusing everyone in the office of wanting him to fail.[83] When the interviewer approached Eugene, he asked if he would be open to making a simple change to the way that he spoke about his current work circumstances, to which he agreed. Together they came up with the word replacement exercise.[84] The interviewer challenged Eugene to use this method for the next five days. During this time, Eugene had to switch any negative words within his phrases to positive ones. For example, instead of stating "Marcus is an assh*le," he would edit the comment to say: "Marcus is an okay guy who needs things to be done correctly."[85] Or, "this place is insane" would be switched to "this place has high standards."[86] This process worked very well in Eugene's favour. He decided to implement this strategy more after the five days had passed. He noticed considerable changes in his mood and experiences within the next three weeks. He no longer felt anxious coming into work, and he came to the realisation that the situations that he was previously stressing about were not as bad as he perceived them to be. He remained in his job and is very happy with his choice.[87]

---

82 Ibid.
83 Ibid.
84 Ibid.
85 Ibid.
86 Ibid.
87 Ibid.

* * *

This makes me smile. Knowing that doing something as basic as rephrasing the way you think and speak about someone can make you smile more each day. This brings me such a degree of comfort, as it can be done with ease and is accessible to everyone.

I hope this chapter has provided all of you with some insightful tips on how to bring more positivity into your life and how your attitude can benefit as a result. To add positivity into your life and work, you can implement so many other methods.

1. A Gratitude Diary: Getting into the habit of writing down ten different things you are thankful for has the potential to change your entire mindset. I've been doing this for the past two years, and it really helps put everything into perspective. Try not to repeat your reasons if you can.
2. Thanking people who have helped you: So many people express their gratitude through direct contact. It usually results in a nice, happy interaction between you and another, making the environment more pleasant. You can't go wrong with this one! Gratitude always wins.
3. Shift your perspective: Play a little game to challenge yourself. Every time you think of a negative thought, try and counteract it with a positive one. You may find yourself appreciating the good more and viewing the situation in a more positive light! For example, being annoyed because you left your credit card at home and now you're only left with cash. The upside to that is now you won't be tempted to spend! It works on everything!

The list is endless, which is a blessing within itself. Congratulations on your new journey of positivity in an empowered style! Remember the words of Lewis Howes: "Life is better when you develop an attitude of gratitude."

CHAPTER 5

SELF-CONFIDENCE

"There will always be someone prettier
There will always be someone smarter
There will always be someone younger
But they will never be you"

—KANYE WEST

SPOTLIGHT ON: YOUNG&BOSSHE
The ability to have faith in yourself and your natural abilities is . . . something I'm admittedly still trying to master ☺.

I would love to be able to say self-confidence is a skill that comes completely naturally to me, but unfortunately it isn't. Much like many other girls in the world, self-confidence is something that has to go through an extensive development stage that can sometimes be lifelong. However, the silver lining in all of this is a lifelong process, but it can be fun if you allow it to be. Building yourself up and listing every reason why you're incredible is amazing. Developing your self-confidence, therefore, seems like a beautiful process, and this chapter is hopefully going to help normalize this whole progression and outline why it should be seen as joyful.

Statistically, 58 percent of college-aged girls feel pressured to be a certain weight, which could be due to a multitude of reasons.[88] Social media appears to be the most common culprit. The pressure to get a certain amount of likes on a picture and have the perfect filter to go with it has falsely given the impression to both men and women of all ages to seek validation through external sources, yet it appears to affect young girls significantly more. Emotional reasons for a lack of confidence may also be a huge contributor. We all go through situations in life that can scar us and impact our self-confidence levels as a result.

* * *

Now let's get on to Young&BosSHE, a female empowerment organization that is a phenomenal form of emotional medicine for a self-confidence boost.

Empowering women and embracing your flaws is at the centre of the Young&BosSHE company. I first came across their site after listening to a podcast they recorded with Caroline Snyder. After listening to a few more episodes, I decided to have a look at their site. I was blown away. The entire site has a distinct welcoming sense of community. From the get-go, they have made it clear all women are welcome to be a part of

---

88 National Association of Anorexia Nervosa and Associated Disorders. "Eating Disorders Statistics." ANAD, accessed July 5, 2020.

their "tribe" as they believe all women deserve "respect and dignity no matter their title, pay grade, or leadership status."[89] This is shown through their blog, which features stories from college students, survivors of eating disorders, and the different experiences of being a woman in the LGBTQ community, to name a few.[90] After seeing all of this, I gained the courage to email them. Since then, I have been fortunate enough to be in contact with Hope, a co-founder of the company who has shared her thoughts with me on the lack of self-confidence in the women of our society.

When it comes to defining self-confidence, Hope agrees with the notion of it being a development process that has no clear and obvious ending. We also share the same opinion on the correlation between social media and self-confidence, and she felt eager to share a personal story that demonstrates why she feels that believing in yourself is so important:

"Self-confidence is a state of mind that's ever-evolving, so few of us truly 'reach' it. There are moments when we feel more confident than others, yes, but it's a journey. It's crucial to foster self-confidence in young girls because our ability to believe in ourselves, encourage ourselves, matters. The ways in which we talk to ourselves and show up for ourselves impact how we see ourselves and the way others see us. Those around us often only believe in our ability to the extent to which we believe in our own. So, the ability to motivate and encourage ourselves, and 'fake it 'til we make it,' is very important. In particular, the

---

[89] Young&BosSHE, "About," Content and Resources for SHEs, by SHEs, November 10, 2019.

[90] Ibid.

rise and use of social media at an increasingly younger age has made it so that girls can compare themselves to one another on a second-by-second basis. It's also created a space where people hide behind the anonymity of the internet to say cruel things. When all you're seeing is everyone else's highlight reel, and all you're hearing is how even your best isn't good enough, it's impossible to believe you are worthy of anything good."

Regarding her general statement on her own practices and actions:

"This happens to me, and so many around me, every day. I notice that it's the times that I convince the Hope inside my head that she is worthwhile, valuable and talented that I see the largest impact on my work and the outcome of whatever I'm working on. It happened today, for goodness' sake! It's not so much the voices of those around me that matter all that much, it's when I actually begin to believe in myself that real change occurs. And that's meaningful to me. I have so many stories I could share here! I see this in the classroom, too. When I encourage my students, it begins to give them the language they need to believe in themselves. But when they start saying those things to themselves, and most importantly, believing them, we see changes in their behaviours and outcomes."

I believe wholeheartedly in the message Hope is trying to spread here. Too many girls exist within our society who are unable to recognize their worth and therefore have low self-confidence as a result. Thankfully, it is an issue that can be rectified with ease over time. Hope's note on how we talk about ourselves is a very good place to start the self-confidence process, as I think it is an issue often overlooked. How many times in your life have you made a simple mistake and decided to mentally "beat yourself up" about it? Perhaps using phrases such as "I'm such an idiot" or "Why am I like this?" Instead of capitalizing on our bad moments, we should imagine we are talking to a young child or a close friend when we are talking to ourselves, as I'm sure we wouldn't be nearly as harsh on them. Not to mention it makes the whole development process slightly more pleasant!

With high self-confidence comes many opportunities. Once young girls start to develop this more empowering mindset, they begin to blossom and take the world by storm. This was another topic Hope and I spoke about, along with how the lack of females in leadership may also be connected to the issue of low self-confidence. To me, Hope and her co-founders embody the principle of believing in yourself. They all have built this amazing platform for themselves where they frequently give women the tools to be unstoppable. In my view, they wouldn't have been able to create that if it wasn't for their belief in themselves and their vision. When we spoke about the company's birth, it felt so authentically down to earth and relatable:

"After graduating from graduate school, our co-founders were all seeking meaningful resources for young professional women that related to professional development, leadership, and more. We had a hard time finding these resources, especially within an inclusive community that advocated for all SHEs, so we built it. Since then, we've met hundreds of other women and femmes who struggle with similar experiences, whether it's the loneliness of marginalization, a lack of leadership development

or female role models, this has only fuelled our passion for what we're doing—empowering young professional SHEs to be self-champions in their leadership through the power of shared experience."

This paired with our discussion on women in leadership and why girls need to start investing in their future from a young age provided a perfect source of urgency and motivation to make a change:

"The old adage that we can only be what we see is true, and if the younger girls around us don't see women in central leadership roles, it's very easy for them to believe they can't serve in those meaningful roles when they grow up. And they absolutely can, and should, be leading right alongside their male peers. Additionally, women should serve in these roles simply because we are qualified to do so. We are good leaders, and we deserve the same level of opportunity to serve as our male counterparts. When we don't see women in these roles as much as we see men, it impacts the way we view all of the men and women around us, even if only subconsciously. By holding central leadership roles, women create a future where we can reach parity and equality in the workplace. Young girls should start thinking about their abilities, their passions, what they love, what excites them, what energizes them, etc. as early as possible, but it's a privilege, frankly, to be able to do that. Some young girls aren't able to focus on these things as survival is their utmost priority. In those situations, it's important for young girls to focus their energy where it is needed. We always want them to know the value of their voices, opinions, spirits and identities."

There is no time like the present. I feel it is crucial for anyone reading Hope's message to take it and run with it. Start making these small changes today. Take a chance on yourself! Enjoy the thrill! Recreating yourself in this way is adventurous and exciting! A new you will bring ample amounts of opportunities!

While I'll admit that my self-confidence is still a work in progress, I feel so much more confident and empowered after hearing exciting and powerful stories and insights like Hope's. Seeing another woman talk openly about her confidence levels rising up throughout the years had inadvertently made my own confidence levels grow. If she can do it, I can do it! I find that having confident role models both around me and in tabloid culture has helped me build up my self-confidence levels significantly. Hearing stories of women who refused to dance to the beat of anyone else's drum, witnessing them be themselves unapologetically is truly empowering. This and making yourself presentable has helped me become more secure without myself. Getting dressed and doing your hair and makeup helps you feel good inwardly as well as outwardly. Here is where the "lead by example" principle comes into play. That is my own personal advice on how to build your confidence. Find someone that has a level of self-confidence that makes them seem on top of the world. It can be someone close to you, or someone that you admire from afar. Use them to be your role model and if possible, ask them how they got to where they are. It will pay off in the long run.

I decided to end the interview by asking Hope if she had a message for any young girls reading this who were struggling with their confidence. This was her response:

"You are valuable. Your voice matters. You matter. Your opinions and stories matter, regardless of any other message you might hear elsewhere, and you have an entire community of women inside Young&BosSHE and beyond that are rooting for you to succeed."

Young&BosSHE represents a new formula of thinking and living for women of the twenty-first century. I have nothing but undeniable respect for the number of lives they are touching, and how much hope and positivity they are bringing into not only the female advancement movement but the world as a whole. It takes such courage to do this, and their success can only mean they are doing something right. Each one of the co-founders is well-established Girl-Bosses, and I am so excited to see what the future has in store for them. I hope they continue to lead the pack for eternity so they can continue to impact not only this generation, but future generations of women.

Action Points for This Chapter:

- Recognise the power that you have within you.
- Realise that you have a family of sisters within your close circle and the feminist movement.
- You are unique. No person on this planet is exactly like you. Embrace that!

CHAPTER 6

FIND THE FUN IN EVERYTHING YOU DO

"Life must be lived by play.
Playing certain games, making many sacrifices, singing and dancing.
And then a man will be able to propitiate the Gods
Defend himself against enemies and win in the contest."

—PLATO

SPOTLIGHT ON: RON CULBERSON

The ancient Stoics taught us that happiness is our responsibility.[91] Being able to take a step back and decide you are truly happy with your life is one of the greatest achievements

---

91   "Responsibility and Response: Why Our Choices Are the Only Thing That Matters," Daily Stoic, November 25, 2017.

you can obtain.[92] Enjoying yourself, having fun, and feeling fulfilled are the best feelings. Within this chapter, I want to discuss the issue of having fun and being successful. Two ideas that are capable of coexisting, yet society has presented them as mutually exclusive. Some of us are very fortunate to be able to do what we love as a career. Others are not so lucky.

We often hear stories about the come up of successful CEOs or leaders who state they've "worked themselves into the ground" to get where they are today along with hearing how painful the journey was to achieve their goals through statements like "I was so stressed out, I considered giving up." I can't help but wonder if these thoughts were present due to the separation between "fun" times and "work" times. We are all constantly told we cannot mix business with pleasure, and to be successful in our careers we must eliminate all the "fun" distractions. I am offering a different message here. Within this chapter, I aim to prove to all the empowered women reading this book that finding the fun in everything you do is the key to getting close to greatness in any sphere. Find what makes you smile, and don't settle for anything less.

* * *

The idea for this chapter came about in such an unconventional and informal way, so much so it is making me smile as I type. It was all inspired by *Modern Family,* one of my favourite shows to binge-watch. It was a Thanksgiving

---

92   Nigel Warburton, *Little History of Philosophy* (Connecticut: Yale University Press, 2014).

episode where an old neighbour, who had made millions from his investment company, told the family he owed all of his success to Phil, who always encouraged him to "find the fun, and follow your heart."[93] This statement lines up with several philosophies (no pun intended) I believe in. In my opinion, having fun is what life is all about. If I'm not finding the joy in something, then I struggle to find its worth. Duchess Meghan agrees with this notion also, as she stated in a recent interview: "It's not enough to just survive something. You've got to thrive. You've got to feel happy."[94] When you're having fun, you feel beautiful, you feel invincible, and most importantly, you feel content. I agree wholeheartedly with both of the notions being put forward by Phil and Meghan. Undeniably, you see the world in a more positive light when you are having fun. Hence, why it is important to seek it out in all areas of your life.

After coming up with the chapter's concept, I went on the hunt for a good book that preached the same message I was hoping to spread. It was nothing but sheer luck that I came across Ron Culberson's *Do It Well. Make It Fun: The Key to Success in Life, Death, and Almost Everything in Between.* Before I go on, I must make a note to say that while this book is about exploring the successes of powerful women and learning how to follow in their footsteps, I believe it is very important to educate young boys and men on how to

---

93 Sandra Gonzalez Updated November 24 and Sandra Gonzalez, "Modern Family Recap: Season 3, Episode 9: Punkin Chunkin," EW.com, 2011, accessed July 5, 2020.

94 Chelsey Sanchez, "Meghan Markle on Royal Life: 'It's Not Enough to Just Survive,'" Harper's BAZAAR (Harper's BAZAAR, October 21, 2019).

empower women along with showing them it is not only possible but crucial to be a part of modern-day feminism and make a difference. Ron's work hit the nail on the head regarding the point I am trying to put forward in this chapter. After a thorough mental debate, I felt it would be a travesty to not include him in this. He may not fit the exact brief of being an empowered *woman*, but he is an excellent role model that everyone can learn from.

His book aims to insert the fun back into the lives of anyone who reads it. It grabs the reader's attention almost immediately and is inclusive to all parts of life, making it more relatable. Ron draws from his personal experiences to explain the formula he has created and how it applies to multiple areas in life.[95] He encourages his audience to try their hardest to "Do Well" in every situation they encounter, and then find all the ways possible to "Make It Fun." In his view, this formula helps to eliminate the chance of failure, since you are now enjoying what you do.

Following up on this, I was even more excited to find an interview Ron had done on his book in *Forbes*. Here he talks about the creation of the book, his life before the book, and how it all came to life:[96]

---

95 RONALD CULBERSON, *Do It Well. Make It Fun: The Key to Finding Balance during Times of Stress, Adulthood, & Death* (Texas: Greenleaf Book Group llc, 2012), accessed July 6, 2020.

96 Dan Schawbel, "Why You Need to Have Fun to Be Successful," Forbes (Forbes Magazine, September 20, 2013).

* * *

He spoke about how he did his graduate thesis in social work and explored the relationship between humour and depression. It was during this time that he realised "humour and fun without excellence can actually work against you, because the credibility is not there."[97] Within his work, he found that if he produced work and it was also fun or funny, it was a lot more effective. This is how his phrase "do it well, make it fun" came into being.[98] He now recommends that if we take each process of our everyday jobs (as he sees jobs as nothing more than a series of processes) and analyse the parts we are not fond of, we have the capability of making it better:

"For instance, I recall a study that said that 85 percent of the people surveyed hated meetings. Well, if meetings are part of our jobs, what are we doing to make them less miserable? We have much more control over our day than we often realize. You can see this whenever you encounter someone in a job that most of us would not want and yet that person has a great attitude. They decided to make the job better."[99]

When asked if he had any advice for anyone who couldn't find a job they enjoyed or was struggling to find the joy in their work, he told a story.

---

[97] RONALD CULBERSON, *Do It Well. Make It Fun: The Key to Finding Balance during Times of Stress, Adulthood, & Death* (Texas: Greenleaf Book Group llc, 2012), accessed July 6, 2020.
[98] Ibid.
[99] Ibid.

The story was about a time that he was forced out of a job that he once enjoyed and had to go into a completely different line of work that he wasn't used to, which was daunting at first.[100] He managed to overcome the adjustment phase and learned to love the job as it enabled him to use the skills that he wasn't aware he had. He also shared the story of a struggling company that used the element of fun and joy to stop them from shutting down:

"I read a great story years ago about a snowshoe company that was struggling. Instead of closing their doors, they took their skill of bending wood and started making furniture. They saw a new opportunity and took advantage of it. The hard thing right now is that normal jobs are harder to come by. The good thing is there has probably never been a better time in our history when there are so many different ways to make a living. So, I believe the goal is to identify the best fit between gifts and skills and the job so that as you pursue new opportunities, you are more likely to get something congruent with who you are. Then, the work becomes much more fulfilling."[101]

I think we can all apply Ron's teaching to everything we do. Finding the fun in mundane tasks adds an element of excitement to our lives and takes the serious element out of it. Have you ever heard the expression, "Don't take life too seriously! It's not like you'll make it out alive?" Just to clarify, I am not encouraging recklessness. Of course, there's a time for fun and games and there is a time to be serious. I just believe the human race needs to add more fun into their

---

100 Ibid.
101 Ibid.

lives. It is a huge benefit to your mental health, and it helps you appreciate your surroundings more. Who wouldn't want that for themselves?!

While I was in the process of writing all of this down and moulding it into a story, I came across a motivational speech about having fun. It was by a motivational speaker named Brendon Burchard, and he encouraged the readers to add a tinge of joy to everything they do.[102]

He stated that he was finally cheerful in his life and feels as if he is having fun all the time.[103] When reflecting on this, he wanted to know how that happens for individuals. He realised that we have to create fun in our lives. The plant doesn't have vitality. It changes and produces vitality. If you need more fun in your life, you're going to have to produce more fun. It's going to take more consideration to purposefully make fun, senseless, crazy, funny, and fair blissful minutes. Joy is capable of arising at any moment, you just have to be fully present to experience it. If you start out every day with the sole intention of being present, Brendon claims to believe that you will unlock the key to discovering funny elements that make you smile in the most small and simple aspects of your life.[104]

We can all find fun elements in the areas we dread the most if we try. For students, every time you make a start on your studying, reward yourself with something small, such as a

---

[102] Brendon Burchard, "How to Bring the Joy to Every Situation," Brendon Burchard, July 27, 2016.
[103] Ibid.
[104] Ibid.

cookie. Do the same when you have finished all your work for the day. This makes the idea of studying worthwhile, as you know you are going to be rewarded for it. Jazzing up your study routine can be done in a lot of different ways! Listening to music or studying with a friend over FaceTime helps a lot! This helped me significantly whenever I was going through an exam period, as it made the whole experience a little bit more entertaining. You won't be doing it alone, and it can make the process a lot easier. In the world of work, you have loads of different ways to do this. For example, the night before work, plan out a nice outfit for the day. Through this, you'll look forward to going into work, and have fun wearing the nice piece you put together. Find a lunch buddy! A daily catch up is something to look forward to as the day goes on, not to mention the pleasure of another person's company. Or, perhaps, plan to do something fun after work so it motivates you to get everything done quickly and efficiently. These things are small, but they can make a big difference in the long run.

I hope it is abundantly clear to everyone that finding the fun elements of every day is essential to getting through life. Loosening up and letting our hair down in places we usually wouldn't provides us with much better experiences. Ron's wise words have had a profound effect on me, and hopefully on you also. Go out and enjoy your life in a joyful Girl-Boss style! Don't settle for less!

Action Points for This Chapter:

- Analyse all of the things that you don't like about your work and think of a way to make it more pleasurable.

- Be present in every moment of your work, look out for the small, fun aspects.
- Plan in advance to reward yourself with small prizes for completing hard tasks, to feel a sense of accomplishment.

CHAPTER 7

STRENGTH AND POWER IN NUMBERS

"We are all equal in the fact that we are different.

We are all the same in the fact that we will never be the same.
We are united by the reality that all colours and cultures are distinct and individual.
We are harmonious in the reality that we are all held to this earth by the same gravity.
We don't share blood, but we share the air that keeps us alive."

—C JOYBELL C

SPOTLIGHT ON: THE #METOO AND #TIMESUP MOVEMENTS

Sisterhood is a concept that reaps the most rewarding benefits once obtained. Nothing feels better than knowing that your best friend has your back, whether that is your Mum, your sister, your cousin, or just a special friend. Female unity in your community can often feel like an extended family, and I feel it's only fair every woman should be able to have this. In recent years, we have been doing very well in regard to displaying the positive power of female unity. We have seen the birth and progression of powerful female movements such as #MeToo and #TimesUp, all promoting the common cause of togetherness.

I believe it is undeniable that women today are fiercely strong and powerful through all sorts of methods. Imagine the power we could harness if we all join forces? The possibilities are endless! We all owe it to ourselves and each other to explore this thoroughly. Together, we can all create a powerful female future and provide a positive, happy, and exciting society for our sisters following in our footsteps. Let's all lead the way, in an empowered style.

After researching the female empowerment movements previously mentioned, I felt so proud of all the progress they have made recently. I was made aware of both the #MeToo and #TimesUp movement a few years back. In my view, the work they have both done is sheer proof of the power women possess when they are united. The #MeToo movement originated in 2006 with Tarana Burke on MySpace.[105] She aimed to bring women who were victims of sexual abuse together and find a way to heal from all the hurt that had occurred.

---

[105] Emma Brockes, "#MeToo Founder Tarana Burke: 'You Have to Use Your Privilege to Serve Other People,'" The Guardian (Guardian News and Media, January 15, 2018).

The movement gained a lot more prominence in 2017 due to the allegations made against Harvey Weinstein.[106] It was then that the hashtag was born. All women around the world who had fallen victim to sexual abuse used the hashtag to show other silent or afraid survivors they were not alone anymore.[107] This sense of togetherness proved to be extremely effective as many high-profile celebrities joined in on the trend.[108] This was the goal of the regime, to change the conversation around sexual abuse and encourage women of all social backgrounds to use their voices to rise. It still holds a huge amount of significance to this day.[109]

The #TimesUp movement was formulated in response to #MeToo along with the Weinstein allegations. The movement has dedicated itself to empowering women to declare that Time's Up on all the injustices that women face and is working to build a future where women can feel secure within themselves: *"We insist upon a world where everyone is safe and respected at work. A world where women have an equal shot at success and security. A world where no one lives in fear of sexual harassment or assault."*[110]

---

106   "Harvey Weinstein Timeline: How the Scandal Unfolded," BBC News (BBC, May 29, 2020).

107   Ibid.

108   Ibid.

109   Joanne Kavanagh, "We Reveal All about #MeToo and the Most Recent Sex Abuse Allegations," The Sun (The Sun, April 18, 2018), accessed July 6th 2020.

110   "About," TIME'S UP Now, accessed June 8, 2020.

The UK division's most current event in London showed the values of the organisation very clearly. Celebrities such as Keira Knightley and Dame Heather Rabbatts came together to celebrate female representation at the BFI London Film Festival.[111] It was through this event I learned about their #4PercentChallenge. Before my research, I had no idea that 4 percent of the top 1,200 studio films were directed by women.[112] The hashtag is trying to increase this figure by encouraging female directors from all backgrounds to employ other women in key behind-the-scenes camera roles. This relates hugely to the organisations' ethos: "An organisation that insists on safe, fair and dignified work for women of all kinds."[113]

The movements seek to build strong elements of solidarity and feels a duty to reinforce the message already being spread worldwide. In short, they are trying to empower and unify women who are on different continents, which is remarkable. What is clear about both of these organizations is they understand the power female organizations are capable of having and have made it their duty to remind these women of this. It brings me a great degree of comfort to know that courageous women in the world are doing their part to ensure that everyone hears this message and that every woman feels welcome to join the fight. Women like this inspire me every day.

---

111 Times Up UK, "TIME'S UP UK Is an Organisation That Insists on Safe, Fair and Dignified Work for Everyone.," Times Up UK, October 2, 1970.

112 Eliana Dockterman, "One Reason Why Oscars Shut Women Out of Best Director," Time (Time, January 13, 2020).

113 Ibid.

The stories that have come to light as a result of these movements have been a true eye-opener. Unfortunately, we have to hear about the trauma some of these women have been through, and it is equally bad for these same women who relive it when sharing their stories. But every cloud has a silver lining.

It is so comforting for all of these women and their audiences to witness the abundance of love, support, and encouragement that comes their way after they share their stories and link themselves to the movement. It confirms the bond of sisterhood and the degree of power I have been referring to. Just a handful of these women choosing to come together and empower one another to share their stories to heal has transformed into a family and has become a blessing to countless women all over the world.[114] This includes women who simply don't feel comfortable sharing their stories but find ease in reading the story of another and finding comfort in the fact they have both been through similar experiences. Regardless of the method, a bond is established and the message is reinforced over and over: You are not alone, we are all connected.

* * *

Below are the stories of Ashley Judd and Drew Dixon, two women who felt the weight of the world was lifted off their shoulders due to the emergence of the movement. Ashley was the first actress in Hollywood to speak openly on Harvey

---

114 Joanne Kavanagh, "We Reveal All about #MeToo and the Most Recent Sex Abuse Allegations," The Sun (The Sun, April 18, 2018).

Weinstein's behaviour.¹¹⁵ Her bravery has gone on to mark her as a respectful heroine in her community:

Ashley stated that the first two emails she received were from official collaborators from the heads of studios.¹¹⁶ I thought that was exceptionally telling since they were ladies who worked for men who were guardians. They were the fastest to send her notes of much thanks and adoration. She thought that the praise would end there, but instead the praise was just beginning. After coming forward, Ashley had people passing her secret notes on aeroplanes thanking her for her bravery of both sexes.¹¹⁷ This reaffirmed that she had done the right thing coming forward and made her proud of her decision.¹¹⁸

Ashley continued to speak out on the details of her lawsuit by saying:

"The power dynamics at play are revealed in a worker's trajectory and her pay check. Being able to have the legal basis for remedy is crucial. The promotion that doesn't materialise, the shift that's reassigned, the opportunities for advantageous overtime . . . those are all ways that women are punished. Bringing that to light and having economic and legal remedies

---

115   Elena Nicolaou, "Ashley Judd Was a #MeToo Heroine Years Before the Movement Began: A Timeline," Timeline of Ashley Judd's Participation In #MeToo, #TimesUp, 2018, accessed July 5, 2020.
116   Ibid.
117   Ibid.
118   Ibid.

is an integral part of the strategy of moving the American workforce forward."[119]

A few months after coming forward, Ashley came across a #MeToo report occurring in the Russian Parliament.[120] This was a very monumental moment for Ashley. She felt an incredible amount of pride knowing that she had helped spark this conversation. Again, it confirmed that she had come forward for the right reasons. It has made her want to "shout from the rooftops" and encourage any victims of sexual assault or harassment to come forward and tell their story.[121]

The story of Drew Dixon has a similar ring. She worked in the music industry and describes how daunting it was to speak out against two famous music icons who had attacked her (one being Russel Simmons), due to their respected status.[122] However, she does not regret her decision, seeing as she has received nothing but praise since doing so, and it has allowed her to slowly get back on track with her career, which she adores:

"The day that story was posted online was one of the most surreal moments of my life. It was like a bomb going off.

---

119 Melena Ryzik et al., "How Saying #MeToo Changed Their Lives," The New York Times (The New York Times, June 28, 2018).

120 Ibid.

121 Elena Nicolaou, "Ashley Judd Was a #MeToo Heroine Years Before the Movement Began: A Timeline," Timeline of Ashley Judd's Participation In #MeToo, #TimesUp, 2018, accessed July 5, 2020.

122 Ibid.

These are incredibly powerful men. They're cultural icons, they're business icons. So just the idea that I was kicking the hornet's nest with these two really huge people, I didn't know what was going to happen. At the very same time, the second I read it, I felt relief because I was done: However scary the reaction and fallout is—even however hard this is for my family to process—I am done carrying this heavy load. It was like a weight had been lifted from my shoulders. I didn't know how heavy it was until I put it down."[123]

Drew elaborated on the difficulty she had with coming forward being a woman of colour.[124] She explained that there are "no heroes to spare" within the black community.[125] Because of this, she didn't want to tear down a black man who was powerful and accomplished. It was this reasoning that kept her from speaking out for twenty-two years.[126] After seeing the significance and impact of #MeToo, she decided that she had to take a stand and be an example to any black women who had been a victim of sexual assault.[127] It was hard, but she realised that she did deserve dignity, respect, and physical safety.

The bravery of these women amazes me. It is not easy to come forward and speak so frankly about issues like this, not to mention the risk of not being taken seriously. They are incredible role models and sources for inspiration. Taking a

---

123 Ibid.
124 Ibid.
125 Ibid.
126 Ibid.
127 Ibid.

giant leap of faith in the hope of uniting the women around you is the mark of a fearless individual. If you haven't experienced this yourself, and there are many women who haven't, count yourself lucky. But it's good to know there is now plenty of support for the unfortunate women who have.

Working together as a community and bringing change forward collectively can be done in a lot of ways. Have you ever heard of the old saying, "birds of a feather flock together?" Go and find your birds! Look for people who think like you. For example, feminists in the making. Always ensure the sisterly bond is created and maintained. Once we all feel we can depend on each other, we will all be unstoppable. Lastly, always advocate for what you believe is right. You were given a voice for a reason. Unified voices will be much louder, and less likely to be ignored. There is strength in numbers, there is confidence in numbers, and there is power in numbers. Break the stimulation, change the future, create a new vision, look back on all of the success and think "She Did That!"

CHAPTER 8

GET OUT OF YOUR COMFORT ZONE!

"If there was one concept that I would suggest to people to take a daily confrontation [of] it is fear.
At that moment all of a sudden where you should be terrified, is the most blissful experience of your life. God placed the best things in your life on the other side of terror. On the other side of your maximum fear are all the best things in life.

—WILL SMITH

SPOTLIGHT ON: DR. BRENÉ BROWN
One of the world's greatest thinkers taught that courage is the most crucial quality a man can possess. He went on to state, "Courage is the first of the human virtues because it makes all others possible."[128] Aristotle was a very wise individual,

---

128 Shafali R. Anand, "Courage Is the First Virtue – Knowledge Is the Second!" The Zen of Learning, February 3, 2010.

and I agree with him wholeheartedly. I'm sure many of us have heard someone around them make a strong statement by saying, "I fear nothing." While this may be true in that person's mind, the reality is every person on this planet is scared of something, whether they are aware of it or not.

Fear is a trait that can manifest itself in many forms. It's something I often wonder if I'll ever overcome. However, I'm willing to try and conquer it slowly but surely. Writing this book is a prime example of this. Taking yourself out of your comfort zone and forcing yourself to do things you wouldn't usually do (within reason of course) adds such a thrill to so many of the experiences we encounter. It will always leave you with an unforgettable memory and an incredible story to tell. Even starting with the small elements of your life can make a huge difference. You can live your best life, as a fearless Girl-Boss.

Before I get on to the remarkable woman who inspired this chapter, I would like to bring a certain song forward that was introduced to me by someone special. I use the term "song" very loosely. Some of you may already be familiar with it due to its popularity on YouTube. The song is called "Everyone's Free to Wear Sunscreen," but I know it as "The Sunscreen Song."[129] One line in the melody has always stuck with me, most likely due to the daunting element of it:

"DO SOMETHING EVERYDAY THAT SCARES YOU."

---

129   Alice Vincent, "'I Wrote It in Four Hours': The Woman Responsible for the Wisdom of Baz Luhrmann's 'Everybody's Free to Wear Sunscreen,' 20 Years On," The Telegraph (Telegraph Media Group, May 29, 2017).

For people who often feel paralyzed by fear, this concept can seem like outright madness. But the philosophy of the song is trying to promote the exact opposite effect. Of course, it isn't trying to encourage you to do things that will cause you harm. Instead, it is encouraging you to not be a victim of fear. The message in this line is to confront fear directly. This is an important message, hence why I felt the urge to include it. Whether we like it or not, we will all be faced with scary situations at some point in our lives. So, trying to avoid it is pointless. Instead, we should embrace it, just as the song is encouraging us.

* * *

Next, I'd like to talk about Dr. Brené Brown, an author, researcher, professor, and well-established boss in her own right. Her work and research have brought her a tremendous amount of success, and her wisdom appears to have no bounds. In 2010, she gave a TED Talk entitled "The Power of Vulnerability" and it remains at number four out of twenty-five in the most popular TED Talks of all time, with over forty-five million views.[130] She has described her research into human empathy as her "calling."[131] However, it was her opinions on fear that captured my attention. During an interview for Oprah's Super Soul Sundays, Brené talked about the different forms of fear and why she feels it is a concept people are getting irritated with:

---

130 Brené Brown, "The Power of Vulnerability," TED, accessed July 6, 2020.
131 Brené Brown, "About," Brené Brown, accessed July 6, 2020.

"Addiction is fear. Eating is fear. Drinking is fear. Drugs are fear. Rage is fear. You know, I drive by big trucks sometimes in Texas, and they have that sticker on the back that says 'Ain't Scared' or something? And I think, 'Love and light to you. You're in so much fear.' We're all afraid. You just have to get to the point where we understand it doesn't mean that we can't also be brave."[132]

She then went on to talk about the presence of fear in our society:

"I think the central question in this country over the last decade is, 'What am I supposed to be afraid of and whose fault is it?' That's the bad news and I think it is has been in every political issue, faith, economic, and social issues. 'What am I supposed to fear and who's to blame?' That gives us something real juicy to do with all this stuff inside of us that we are uncomfortable with. . . . so people buy into it because they feel fear and they don't have the language to attach what it is. The good news is, I really believe, and I'm an optimistic person but I believe, even as a researcher, we're at a really important tipping point. I think people are sick and tired of being afraid."[133]

What I love most about Dr. Brown's message is that it offers a renewed sense of hope. She talks about how being bold and being fearful are factors that are capable of being mutually exclusive, a concept I had not thought about previously.[134]

---

132   Frances Bridges, "5 Ways to Be Brave According to Brené Brown's Netflix Special 'The Call To Courage,'" Forbes (Forbes Magazine, April 30, 2019).
133   Ibid.
134   Ibid.

Additionally, the idea of fear in the form of passing blame on others in positions of power was something that I found to be intriguing.[135] It is good to know she believes that people will start to rise against their fears. It gives us a glimmer of hope for the future. During a more recent interview of Super Soul Sundays, Dr. Brown divulged into the mental aspect of fear and provided Oprah's listeners with a unique method to reassure yourself if you feel your fears (in the form of anxiety) are leading you down a path of irrationality.[136] Have you ever been in a crucial social moment such as a first date or an interview and left the situation thinking "Oh no that was awful! What will they think of me now?!" Well, so has Dr. Brown. Here is her view on it:

"We all do it. I mean, if you and I finish this interview, and we walk down the hill and I say, 'Thanks a lot! I really appreciate you,' and go like this . . . (sigh), My brain takes that as anxiety or fear, and I immediately make up a story. 'I knew she never liked me. I didn't do the right thing. It was terrible.' All of a sudden, I'm working up a whole narrative. Wow. And then, you know, it just keeps going and going. So how do we make sure that or know the story that we're telling ourselves isn't in alignment with what did happen. Yeah, the first thing I have to do is when you look at me like that, and I feel something in response to it, you have to acknowledge, 'Woah. A button has been pushed.' I've been hooked . . . something emotional is happening here, I'm responding. And then I have to be willing to get curious about what it is. So instead of immediately going

---

135   Ibid.
136   Brené Brown, "Dr. Brené Brown Archives," SuperSoul.tv, accessed July 7, 2020.

into my crazy story . . . I have to go to . . . Okay. I'm emotionally hooked around something that is happening outside."[137]

This is something we can all benefit from. I'm sure we are all guilty of coming up with the most outrageous conclusions at times and we somehow can justify it to ourselves mentally. This method is an attempt at stopping that from happening. We sometimes just have to take a step back from the situation and try and put ourselves in the mind of an outsider to rationalize everything.

* * *

One of Dr. Brown's most famous works is her book *Daring Greatly*.[138] People who have read it have found it astonishing and described it as "all the navigation you'll ever need."[139] The book aimed to help everyone recognize the power of their vulnerability and how it can improve your methods of living, learning, parenting, and much more. It is now recognized as a *New York Times* best-seller, and I can understand why.[140] This book has so many incredible moments in it, so I struggled to pinpoint a single extract to share here!

---

137 Breaking News, Dr. Brené Brown is on SuperSoul today talking about transcending failure and RISING STRONG, November 12, 2017, video, 43m27s.

138 Brene Brown, *Daring Greatly: How the Courage to Be Vulnerable Transforms the Way We Live, Love, Parent, and Lead.* New York: Avery, 2012.

139 Ibid.

140 Gary Chapman et al., "Love and Relationships Books – Best Sellers – Dec. 11, 2016," The New York Times (The New York Times, 2016).

Instead, I've decided to put my favourite quotes from the book below, as they will be easier to remember, and therefore have a bigger impact.

"I define vulnerability as uncertainty, risk and emotional exposure. With that definition in mind, let's think about love. Waking up every day and loving someone who may or may not love us back, whose safety we can't ensure, who may stay in our lives or may leave without a moment's notice, who may be loyal to the day they die or betray us tomorrow—that's vulnerability."[141]

"Vulnerability is not weakness, and the uncertainty, risk, and emotional exposure we face every day are not optional. Our only choice is a question of engagement. Our willingness to own and engage with our vulnerability determines the depth of our courage and the clarity of our purpose; the level to which we protect ourselves from being vulnerable is a measure of our fear and disconnection."[142]

"We live in a world where most people still subscribe to the belief that shame is a good tool for keeping people in line. Not only is this wrong, but it's dangerous. Shame is highly correlated with addiction, violence, aggression, depression, eating disorders, and bullying."[143]

---

[141] Brené Brown, Daring Greatly: How the Courage to Be Vulnerable Transforms the Way We Live, Love, Parent, and Lead. New York: Avery, 2012.
[142] Ibid.
[143] Ibid.

God bless Dr. Brené Brown for sharing all of her wisdom on vulnerability as a fear that can easily be overcome with time. It gives us all more of a reason to go ahead and push ourselves to be more daring and free without even considering our fears. It has been said by many that we grow the most when we are uncomfortable. From this point onward, I am calling on all the Girl-Bosses reading this book to go ahead and listen to Dr. Brown's TED Talk on vulnerability and use it as a force of inspiration. In addition to this, I sincerely hope this chapter encourages you to find your way of doing something that scares you once in a while. Whether that is applying for a job you think you'll never get or asking out your long-term crush. Or, even something simpler such as dining out alone, or attending a dance class you've always wanted to do but have been too scared to try. Be willing to try anything that forces you out of your comfort zone. I hope it makes you a stronger, more confident, and unstoppable woman. Or, as I like to phrase it, an empowered woman in the making.

Action Points for This Chapter:

- Do something each day that scares you.
- Embrace the unknown, with the hope that you might find out more about yourself.
- Always try and rationalise your wild conclusions when you are in the moment.

CHAPTER 9

SELF-LOVE

---

*"How You Love Yourself Is
How You Teach Others
To Love You."*

—RUPI KAUR

SPOTLIGHT ON: EMMA GREDE

Love is seen as this magical concept that has the power to make you glow. It has been described as an instant feeling of joy that makes you feel like you are walking on air. You become obsessed with the other person in your relationship, and you cannot get enough of each other.

Imagine feeling that way from loving yourself?

Self-love is one of the most rewarding gifts you will ever give to yourself. Becoming your own best friend is beyond comforting, and it makes you feel so much more comfortable within your skin. Have you ever heard the expression: "You cannot expect anyone else to love you if you do not love yourself"? I agree with this expression wholeheartedly. Life became so much easier for me once I learned to not only love myself, but to be kind to myself on a regular basis. We should all aim to treat ourselves as we would treat our best friend. I hope this chapter can inspire you all to work toward having a better relationship with yourselves.

* * *

The person I want to bring to the spotlight in this chapter is Emma Grede. Emma is a UK ambassador for Women for Women International (WFWI) and sits on the global board of directors.[144] You may have seen Emma's face before, since she is a fashion entrepreneur. In 2016, she launched Good American with Khloe Kardashian, a denim brand that has expanded into athleisure wear, maternity wear, and much more.[145] The message of unifying and empowering women to love and appreciate their appearance (feel your best through looking your best) is at the centre of their company's values.[146]

I was very impressed when I discovered her connection to WFWI, as it showed the versatility in her career. Emma has achieved a great deal in her career with some notable highs.

---

144 "Emma Grede: Women for Women International," TWICE the impact for women survivors of war, accessed July 3, 2020, accessed July 5th 2020.

145 Elana Lyn Gross, "How Emma Grede And Khloe Kardashian Are Building Their Size-Inclusive Fashion Line Good American," Forbes (Forbes Magazine, June 3, 2019).

146 Ibid.

But what strikes me the most about her is her ambition to encourage all women to love themselves, and how she has chosen to do this through the medium of fashion. The method is so unorthodox, yet so effective! When I was in the very early stages of this writing journey, I really wanted to include different women and charities that went out of their way to make a positive impact on the world along with helping people who were less fortunate than themselves. To me, Women for Women exceeds this definition.

They quite literally change the lives of women who live in countries that have been affected by conflict or war and assist them with the necessary tools to rebuild their lives in the best way possible. After learning that around fifty thousand Bosnian women were being victimised on a daily basis as a weapon of war, in addition to their homes being destroyed, Zainab Salbi decided to found Women for Women International to help put a stop to all of this injustice. Zainab and these women who work within the organisation are exceptional.[147] It still amazes me that Zainab created this whole establishment at the age of twenty-three.[148] I'm sure even she couldn't have believed her company would achieve the amount of success it has generated over the past few years.

Emma has been involved with the organization since 2008 and is very passionate about her work there, as the values of sisterhood and helping others are very close to her heart.[149] In an interview with Brita Fernandez-Schmidt, Emma spoke

---

147 "Our Story," Women for Women International, accessed July 3, 2020.
148 Ibid.
149 Ibid.

about her background and how it inspired her to get into feminism along with the mentors she had in her life and how she helps bring an element of togetherness to the women that surround her.

"Since I've moved to the US, I've been surrounded by this idea of mentorship and wondered, 'Who are my mentors?' Because nobody labelled themselves as such. But I did have them, and I was definitely lucky that I'd been in female-founded businesses, and then as I've come up in the industry I've found many women who have championed me."[150]

Emma also shared her methods of unifying other women. She is a believer of karmic effect and believes if you help a fellow sister, it will come back to you in full force, along with demonstrating the importance of showing love to those around you in an effort to love yourself.[151]

"I think, personally, when I'm struggling, when I'm having a difficult time, as you inevitably do, I always think to myself, 'What can I do to help someone else?'" For Emma, it is as simple as going through a list of three options to reach out to another person and show them love. *"I can make a phone call, I can send an email, I can hook this person up with this person, etc. There's this magical way that it will come back to me [in the future]."*[152]

---

150 WomenForWomenUK, "Brita Fernandez-Schmidt and Emma Grede discuss the power of feminism in Facebook Live Chat," May 21, 2018, video, 26m24s.

151 Ibid.

152 Ibid.

Growing up in East London, Emma was surrounded by community and learned its value in her life and the lives of others.[153] She has taken these life lessons and applied them to her time with WFWI in hopes that it will inspire women to see how lifting one another is, in turn, lifting us all.[154] Her efforts within the feminist movement are focused on connection and the idea that no woman is alone. This sense of togetherness enforces the message of love and acceptance both for yourself and others around you. Community helps build our character to a certain degree.

Emma's clothing brand, Good American, continues on this idea of connection and empowerment. I was made aware of the brand through an episode of *Keeping up with the Kardashians,* one of my favourite guilty pleasures. Both Emma and Khloe spoke openly about wanting to help women learn how to love their shape and change the way the fashion world viewed plus-sized women. During the episode, the women were shocked to find out during one of their press interviews that they had to sell 150,000 units to breakeven.[155] Luckily, they had nothing to worry about as the launch was the second biggest event in the history of Nordstrom's and everything sold out in the process. They made one million dollars that day alone. [156]

---

153 Ibid.

154 Ibid.

155 Keeping up with the Kardashians, "Kim's Last Ditch Effort," PrimeVideo, 43m45s, April 2, 2017.

156 Jen Nurick, "Khloe Kardashian's Good American Denim Line Made USD $1 Million in Its First Day," Vogue Australia, January 16, 2018.

During a separate interview, Emma spoke more about how her passion led to the formation of the company and how it became the basis for why she and Khloe felt obligated to fulfil this mission:

"In the beginning, we felt like we were on a mission, and we were really excited about what that was. We then decided that it was denim, and then it could be lots of other things. But it was really more about 'what is our intent?' And our intent was really to service these women who really felt under-serviced by the fashion industry."[157]

This interview made me think about the whole fashion industry in a different light. Without even realising it, most clothing brands and fashion names choose to hire women with a slim physique, which sends the unconscious message that those types of girls are the definition of "beautiful" or "attractive." I think it is great that Emma and Khloe both recognised that this choice of model can lead to women having a lack of self-love and wanted to change that as soon as they could. Their brand is encouraging women to be comfortable in their skin and love themselves in the process. This is a crucial message for so many women of every age. They are telling us all to love ourselves regardless of what society may be projecting.

---

157 Ibid.

* * *

To me, Emma Grede is the perfect example of a modern-day feminist. Her inspirational words are so crucial and educational. This interview made her feel a lot more relatable, whether that's because of her down-to-earth nature, or simply because she's a Londoner! Either way, her words on having female mentors and supporting each other in both good and bad times are all good ways to create a community for ourselves. Being your companion's strength is important when they feel they have none. Feeling like we have someone to depend on, understanding your self-worth, and loving yourself unconditionally are all very important. Family values are crucial for our family of Girl-Bosses. So, having Emma's advice here can be a foundation to build upon. Slowly but surely, we can make our way there, through teamwork and admiration.

I recently found a story on the *Huffington Post* that relates to Emma's mission. A woman named Fernanda was talking about one of Deepak Chopra's spiritual laws named The Law of Detachment.[158] I really admired the parts where Fernanda shared how she learned to fall in love with herself and decided to put that love over anything and everything else she had going on within her life. She speaks about how she wanted to find the love of her life so urgently but wasn't having much luck. So instead, she decided to apply self-love and see where it took her:

---

158 Fernanda Lodeiro, "The Secret Spot Where I Found Love: A Lesson in the Law of Detachment," HuffPost (HuffPost, February 9, 2015).

"I decided that with or without a special one I could and SHOULD be happy. I began dating myself, practicing extreme self-care, and nourishing myself in a loving way. I would take walks on Sunday mornings in gorgeous neighbourhoods in Buenos Aires like Palermo and Recoleta. I would visit the arts and crafts markets and get myself treasures. I continued to dance tango not to find anyone, but because I loved it (and because embraces are always nourishing!). On the weekends I would take day trips outside the city to get closer to nature. I would go to concerts on my own when I couldn't find a friend to go with and that was perfect. I would cook healthy, nourishing meals for myself and experiment with new recipes for my friends. I learned to appreciate good wines, music, and candles. Life became so rich and fun! I was totally in love: with myself, with my life, with things just as they were."[159]

Once this self-love mindset had become second nature to Fernanda, she decided to accept an invitation to her high-school reunion. She reunited with her high-school love, who she had admired for so many years.[160] After catching up, they exchanged numbers and got married one year later. Fernanda believes that loving herself was the one key element she was missing. She describes it as "the missing piece in the puzzle.[161] Once it is found, everything will be put into place."

You can apply self-love to yourself in many ways. Today it often falls under the category of self-care, which is a form of love also. Self-care Sunday has become very popular within

---

159   Ibid.
160   Ibid.
161   Ibid.

the last few years. You could treat yourself at the end of every week! Have that glass of wine, buy that bag that you've wanted for ages, take a nice hot bath, apply a face mask, whatever you need to do to show your appreciation to yourself. See it as a reward! A treat for the week if you will! Congratulate yourself for getting to the end of the week! Seek it out and apply it generously!

Action Items for This Chapter:

- Love yourself wholeheartedly, no matter the cost.
- Get to know yourself better! Make you sure to do one thing that makes you smile each day.
- Trust the process. Understand that this is the key to unlocking your best life.

CHAPTER 10

MAKE YOUR MARK IN HISTORY

"Your Mind Has The Intellect To Lift The World
Your Heart Has The Wisdom To Better The World
And Your Soul Has The Genius To Elevate The World."

—MATSHONA DHLIWAYO

SPOTLIGHT ON: KOFFEE

Creating a name for yourself in the world is an extremely admirable task. It is not something that is done with ease. We are very fortunate in today's age to be surrounded by a large number of women who have successfully made their mark in history and will forever be remembered as the people who changed the game. Women such as Maya Angelou, Marie Curie, Michelle Obama, and Hillary Clinton are a few names that come to mind instantly. In this chapter, I want to shine a light on a young woman who has managed to make her mark in the music industry, simultaneously breaking world records, while making it all look easy (which it is not).

So logically, the next question is obvious: How do I make my mark on the world? Judging by all of the women that have managed to achieve this distinction, I am going to phrase this as simply and memorably as I know to be possible: Be good at what you do.

Have you ever heard the expression, "whatever you are, be a good one"? That is what needs to be applied here, as simple as it may seem. Every single one of the women I mentioned above is considered an expert in their field and it has made them more memorable as a result. Maya Angelou had an incredible way with words and was extremely effective when it came to advocating for Civil Rights.[162] Marie Curie was considered a top-level scientist, hence why she was able to give such life changing contributions in the fight to cure cancer.[163] Michelle Obama's work and service as First Lady of the United States for eight years has made her one of the most popular First Ladies to date.[164] Last, but certainly not least, Hillary Clinton was elected as the first female senator in New York and won the popular vote during her campaign in the 2016 Presidential election because she is considered to

---

162   "Maya Angelou," Academy of Achievement, November 7, 2019.
163   Marie Curie, "Marie Curie the Scientist: Biog., Facts & Quotes," Marie Curie, 2020, accessed July 6, 2020.
164   "Michelle Obama Popularity Polls: Washington Post," The Washington Post (WP Company, 2016), accessed July 6, 2020.

be a boss in her field (or a Girl-Boss if we are being specific).[165] The proof is in the pudding, ladies.

In the summer of 2019, people all around the globe fell in love with the musical stylings of Koffee, a nineteen-year-old young woman whose music never fails to put me in a good mood. In 2020, she won her first Grammy award, which placed her as the first woman to win a Grammy in the "Best Reggae Album" category.[166] After reflecting upon how much I have grown to love her music, I felt it was only fair to feature her in this book, as she defines what it means to be a Girl-Boss in the twenty-first century. Koffee's music offers such a different sound that is soothing to the ear. She is able to make her songs so joyful and catchy. You can't help but bop and sway along with the song as it plays. The positivity that radiates from all of her songs is what makes her stand out as an artist. I feel so happy for everything she has achieved, and not including her in this book would have been a tragedy. Koffee has effortlessly made a name for herself and will go down as one of the most memorable reggae artists to date as a result. I could not be prouder of her.

Koffee would not have gotten this far if she was not recognized as the musical genius that she is. Her gift is very rare, and I think the world is now starting to acknowledge and appreciate this. In many places within the world, it isn't very

---

165   History.com, "Hillary Clinton Is Elected to the U.S. Senate," History.com (A&E Television Networks, July 24, 2019).

166   Elias Leight, "Koffee Makes History with Grammy Win, Signs With RCA," Rolling Stone (Rolling Stone, February 7, 2020).

common to hear reggae music in the music charts.[167] It is typically associated with the Caribbean and tends to stay in that bracket. However, Koffee has managed to allow the reggae genre to spread its wings once more and be enjoyed throughout the world by everyone, showing how major her success has been.

Koffee, born Mikayla Simpson, is from Spanish Town, Jamaica, and has always had a special love for music.[168] She taught herself how to play the guitar at the age of twelve and has stated that her number one musical inspiration was the reggae artist Protoje.[169] After performing in a high school talent show, Koffee believed she had the confidence to actively pursue a career in music. She began to gain popularity after writing and releasing a song entitled "Legend," which she dedicated to Usain Bolt, who went on to repost the song on his Instagram page.[170] Within a year from this, she was signed by Columbia Records and released her first EP "Rapture."[171] I truly admire the way Koffee has been able to make such a prominent name for herself at such a young age in an industry that is famously competitive. Her songs have the reoccurring theme of being positive, grateful, and thankful to God and all of the people around you. This is seen in her most famous song to date along with her comments in

---

167 S. Leslie, "Koffee Youngest Reggae/Dancehall Artist to Top Billboard Chart," Urban Islandz, April 1, 2019.
168 Reggaeville, "Biography: Koffee," www.reggaeville.com, 2020, accessed July 6, 2020.
169 Ibid.
170 Ibid.
171 Ibid.

interviews, where she constantly repeats the phrase, "Gratitude is a must."[172] I truly believe she exhibits a different kind of sound because her lyrics have such a strong meaning. Her positive messages have served her very well and it is amazing to witness. I cannot stress enough how important it is to have more music like this in the charts (in my view). Singing about gratitude and positivity is bound to make a more profound effect on the lives of everyone.

When asked about her humble personality in an interview with Apple Music, Koffee shrugged it off as a natural trait of her personality, talking about how fame has changed her as a person. [173]

Koffee has attributed her positive outlook and attitude of gratitude to her mum. Her influence has not only shaped who Koffee is as a person but, in turn, encouraged her music to hold the same energy.

Koffee's passion was not always music. In an interview with *The Voice,* she shared that her dream career was to become a pharmacist, a career that could not be more different from what she does now.[174] It was so interesting to hear her speak, and talk about how none of what she achieved was originally in her "life-plan" and how she had always wanted to be a

---

172 Ibid.
173 Apple Music, "Koffee on Apple Music," Apple Music, 2020, accessed July 6, 2020.
174 Leah Sinclair, "Koffee Talks on Her Life Changing, Influences, Toast, Throne and More," Voice Online, June 17, 2019.

singer when she was younger but lost sight of the vision.175 She was raised in an Adventist church, so she was always surrounded by musical stylings. She developed her love for reggae music when she turned fourteen.176 The flow, style, and lyrics entranced her to the point of inspiration. One day, she said to herself "I think I want to try this." Not long after this, she found out that she was not accepted into sixth form, a blessing in disguise.177 Although these are two high school grades that are optional, she was very disheartened by the outcome. This is what pushed her to pursue a musical career. She wrote her first song called "Burning," which directly speaks to the situation of not getting into sixth form. She says, "Meh come with the fire. No matter what, nothing can out my flame. I'm still here and I'm going to burn somewhere else."178

What I love the most about Koffee's story is how much she believes in herself. She didn't allow a major setback to get in the way of her being a superstar, which is a lesson that so many of us can learn from. She never stopped believing in her abilities and has come such a long way because of that.

I have often wondered what I want to do to leave my mark on the world. I feel lucky because I am still in the "figuring-it-out" phase of my life. I still have a lot of time to decide. This book is definitely my first step in doing so. I am writing this book with the hope that you will feel encouraged to go and find a way to change the course of history. I want you to

---

175 Ibid.
176 Ibid.
177 Ibid.
178 Ibid.

use this as your fuel, your motivation, and your driving force, however you want to define it. Go out there and do it. It might be daunting, but if I can find the courage to write this book with the hopes of it improving the lives of all young girls in the world, you can do and find whatever you are passionate about, and be remembered for it.

So, that sums it all up! To make your mark in history, you must be good at what you do. Follow in the example of Koffee and any of the other women mentioned in this chapter, or someone who personally inspires you, whether they are famous or not. Having the simple desire of wanting to do good for the world is an amazing first step. The next step is just figuring out what method you will adopt to do so. Koffee is a physical reminder of this theory being accurate. Whether it is through music, arts, education, or anything else, you can make your mark on the world. You can inspire millions. It is all possible through faith.

Action Points for This Chapter:

1. Pay close attention to what you want to do with your life.
2. Go and live your truth. You never know who you will be inspiring in the process.
- Work hard to ensure that you are remembered for what you have achieved.

CHAPTER 11

STEP, EMPOWER, AND UPLIFT EACH OTHER

―

"You may shoot me with your words
You may cut me with your eyes
You may kill me with your hatefulness
But still, like air, I rise."

—MAYA ANGELOU.

SPOTLIGHT ON: MEGHAN, THE DUCHESS OF SUSSEX
The ability to empower the people that surround you regardless of the circumstances is considered to be a superpower in today's age. From the historic 1943 wartime poster of Rosie the Riveter entitled "We Can Do It!" to the recent #MeToo movement of 2017, there appears to be an energy that surrounds women to uplift, support, and empower one another more frequently. To possess this trait is to possess a rare gift. The ability to empower others is an attribute that separates the strong from the weak, the courageous from the timid,

and singles out the people who will go down in history for reintroducing bravery into generation after generation.

A woman I believe not only possesses the amazing qualities I have listed above but also prides herself on acting upon empowerment with every second she lives is none other than the Duchess of Sussex. I have been a fan of Duchess Meghan from the moment she announced her engagement to Prince Harry in 2017.[179] Her indestructible passion for promoting female empowerment along with her sheer dedication to advocating for the issues of gender inequality plays a huge role in the inspiration of this book.

Meghan's ability to be so relatable and down to earth speaks volumes as to why she is adored internationally. She is a woman who has proven on multiple occasions that she is not just a pretty face. I believe when an individual puts their heart and soul into supporting causes they care about, it opens the door to create an open space for people to not only love you but to hold you in high regard eternally. Duchess Meghan is a modern-day princess and a dynamic Girl-Boss.

The day I listened to a speech I now refer to as "The Meghan Empowerment Talk" was a day I will never forget. The world watched in wonder as the Duke and Duchess of Sussex carried out their ten-day tour of South Africa, but it was the last official day that struck a chord in my heart. I saw on their Instagram page that Meghan had aimed her last speech at the young people of the world. After listening and rereading

---

179 S Null, "Prince Harry And Meghan Markle's Engagement: Everything You Need to Know," Grazia (Grazia, January 29, 2018).

her words, I felt so connected to her as a woman and so empowered to do my part in making the world a more positive place to inhabit. The Duchess connected well with every young person that was in the room directly by saying, "This is for you." Whilst keeping her eyes on the audience, she continued to say, "In a world that can seem so aggressive, confrontational, and dangerous, you should know that you have the power to change it. Because whether you're here in South Africa, at home in the UK, the US, or around the world, you actually have the power to change things, and that begins with how you connect to others."[180]

It was these words that made me discover the true meaning of the so-called "Meghan Effect," which is what I view as her unconscious method of empowering her audience by connecting with them on a personal and relatable level. Whether you are in the room with her, hearing her speak on the television, or hearing about the encounters she has had with different organizations, Meghan has a way of silencing out the rest of the world and making you feel as if it is just you and her having a discussion. The connection she makes with her audience has the effect of making you feel very in tune with her while she is speaking.

During her travels to Africa and beyond, she continued to captivate the audience and confirm this relatable bond I am referring to by saying: "I have learned from the people I've met here, that whether it's about society's expectation of masculinity or femininity, or how we divide ourselves by race or

---

180 Prince Harry & Duchess Meghan Final Day Royal Tour Africa 2019! *Inc Speeches! YouTube*, 2019.

faith or class or status—everyone has value, and everyone deserves to be heard and respected. And if you live your life in that way, your generation will start to value each other in ways the rest of us have not yet been able to do." The applause from the room was profound, and the "Meghan Effect" was felt around the globe.

I couldn't help but notice while listening, the Duchess may have been referencing her personal experience of being a target of racism, disrespect, and global bullying recently.[181] This was a large part of the reason why I felt the need to include Meghan within this book. She has recently spoken out in the press about how she believes vulnerability should be seen as one of the greatest strengths a human can possess.[182] I agree that to be vulnerable is to present yourself as an open target and be subjected to judgmental attacks from the people that surround you. So, the decision Meghan has made to take that vulnerability and use it as a form of empowerment is something I have watched from afar and admired significantly.

Being the eager "Meghanist" (a term that many "Sussex Squad" members have been using to refer to themselves on Twitter) that I have become over the past year, I was thrilled when I saw that both Harry and Meghan had filmed a documentary while on their South African tour.[183] I was very excited

---

181   Kayleigh Dray, "Caroline Flack Inspired Us to Be Kind. Why Can't We Do That with Meghan?" Stylist (Stylist, February 29, 2020).

182   Bryony Gordon, "Behind the Scenes with Meghan Markle: Duchess Tells Bryony Gordon How Vulnerability Is One of Humanity's Greatest Strengths," The Telegraph (Telegraph Media Group, October 31, 2019).

183

to see them both talk in such a candid manner regarding their personal lives, something that is an extreme rarity for members of the Royal Family. The documentary ended on a very powerful note. An open conversation between Meghan and the interviewer, Tom Bradby, allowed everyone to see a very human side of the Duchess, as we all learned of the struggles and pressures she has been forced to endure upon her marriage into the British Monarchy.[184] Seeing Meghan so emotional and close to tears made me empathise with her deeply. I evidently was not the only person who felt this way either, since the hashtag #WeLoveYouMeghan was trending at number one in the UK and number two in the US after the documentary was released.[185]

Meghan's entry into the British Royal Family caused a lot of people to recognise her as a devout feminist. However, before this, she was advocating the same way for female rights and working with major organisations. Before becoming a Duchess, Meghan worked very closely with UN Women and humanitarian relief. Her speech at the UN Women conference in 2015 was widely praised and placed Meghan in a very complimentary light. I remember watching the speech after learning of Meghan's engagement to Prince Harry. I watched the speech in awe. The confidence and ease that she had with public speaking in addition to the powerful stories

---

184 Bonnie McLaren, "ITV's Tom Bradby Explains How He Found a 'Bruised and Vulnerable' Prince Harry and Meghan Markle," Grazia (Grazia, October 24, 2019).

185 Amelia Wynne, "#WeLoveYouMeghan: Outpouring of Support for Duchess of Sussex," Daily Mail Online (Associated Newspapers, October 20, 2019).

and statements she was making throughout the speech made me think, "Wow. She will be incredible with the job side of her new role." Meghan's speech focused on gender inequality within the world. After telling the touching story of her disagreement with a TV advertisement as a child, Meghan began to speak of different statistics that she found to be equally disappointing.[186] She announced that the elimination of gender inequality won't be possible until 2095. She also stated that the percentage of women's political participation and leadership of female parliamentarians globally has only increased by 11 percent since 1995, to which she responded with, "Come on. This has to change."[187] Even though she was using such simple, colloquial language, her words were extremely empowering. It makes you want to go and make a change for the better. This is a trait of an incredible leader in my eyes.

Meghan's dedication to empowering other young women within the world is reflected very strongly within her patronages here within the UK. Her work with the Queen's Commonwealth Trust works directly with empowering and funding the young leaders who are aiming to create a brighter future for the world. Meghan has used her position as vice president of the organisation to encourage young women to use their voices to directly impact change.[188] The most notable examples of this was her appearance on a panel for

---

186 Meghan Markle, "The Girl Power Speech That Put Meghan Markle on the Map," *The Sydney Morning Herald,* October 9, 2018.

187 Ibid.

188 "The Queen's Commonwealth Trust," The Queen's Commonwealth Trust, 2020, accessed July 6, 2020.

International Women's Day in 2019 at King's College London, and her round table discussion on gender inequality with The QCT and One Young World alongside her husband, Prince Harry. She works endlessly to ensure that every young girl who listens to her speeches is filled with encouragement, in the hopes that she will go out into the world to be a change maker.[189] It is so important to have modern-day Princesses within our society, as their level of influence is incredible. It is so comforting to know that we have Meghan being a beacon of hope for young women worldwide.

The Duchess of Sussex is a powerhouse for uplifting and empowering women on a global scale. She has openly shown that being at a low point within your life isn't an excuse to stop being a force of positivity within the world, along with giving countless women one thousand reasons why they should smile. Not only does she execute this, but she is highly successful in doing so. We all can do little things to empower one another if we make an effort to: just doing the simple things, like telling a friend who is going through a hard time that she is doing well, or buying a gift for someone who has been feeling underappreciated, or just telling someone they are beautiful. Small things such as this can make such a difference in someone's day, hence why we must practice this more often.

Meghan is a huge part of why this book has come to life because to me, she clearly defines what it means to be a Girl-Boss. She is intelligent, she is thought provoking, she has a heart of gold, and she deeply cares about making the world a

---

189 Ibid.

better place for all of us. Throughout everything she undergoes, she never fails to have a huge smile on her face and carry out her role as a Duchess with utter grace, while reminding us of the importance of being there for one another. I am so proud to describe Meghan as a true inspiration, a role model, and most importantly, an undeniable global icon.

Action Points for This Chapter:

- Always be a beacon of hope and change for everyone who surrounds you. You never know who you will be inspiring in the process.
- Find an injustice that doesn't sit right with you and empower others around you to take a stand for the greater good.
- Recognise the power of your voice. If not you, then who?

CHAPTER 12

FIND YOUR PASSION

"You can do anything as long as you have:
The Passion
The Drive
The Focus
& The Support."

—SABRINA BRYAN

SPOTLIGHT ON: LILLY SINGH

We are coming to the end of this book now. At this point, I'm sure you've all picked up on my love for quotes. Life passions are a subject that contains an abundance of quotes, much to my delight! A very famous one associated with the topic comes from Marc Anthony, who stated, "If you do what you love, you'll never work a day in your life."[190] His words seem so true in so many ways. It is an underrated blessing to be able to honestly say that you love what you do for a living and

---

190   Marc Anthony, "Marc Anthony Quotes," BrainyQuote (Xplore, 2020), accessed July 6, 2020.

truly enjoy going into work every day. To achieve this, you must put a lot of faith and trust into your instincts and follow your passions, which this chapter will aim to explore. Doing what you believe is your calling in life has proven to reap unbelievable benefits for everyone who has followed their passions. One of the main reasons why I chose to embark on writing this book was because I have always had a passion for writing, so this felt like the next logical step in following that passion. I have loved every step of the process wholeheartedly. We all have our passions—it is just about finding them and refusing to let them go that counts for everyone.

Before I go ahead and introduce the star of this chapter, I want to just share a quick speech I found very inspiring while listening to a song many years ago called "Live Life Now." Before the song starts, a speech by Alan Watts booms, clearly telling a very inspiring story about chasing the things that excite you in life rather than settling for the ordinary:

"What makes you itch? What sort of a situation would you like?

Let's suppose, I do this often in vocational guidance of students, they come to me and say, well, 'We're getting out of college and we haven't the faintest idea what we want to do.' So, I always ask the question, 'What would you like to do if money were no object? How would you really enjoy spending your life?'

Well, it's so amazing as a result of our kind of educational system, crowds of students say well, we'd like to be painters, we'd like to be poets, we'd like to be writers, but as everybody knows you can't earn any money that way. Or another person says well, I'd like to live an out-of-doors life and ride horses.

I said, 'You want to teach in a riding school? Let's go through with it. What do you want to do?'

When we finally got down to something, which the individual says he really wants to do, I will say to him, you do that and forget the money, because, if you say that getting the money is the most important thing, you will spend your life completely wasting your time. You'll be doing things you don't like doing in order to go on living, that is to go on doing things you don't like doing, which is stupid.

And so, therefore, it's so important to consider this question: What do I desire?"[191]

The message Alan is putting forward here is so important. It captures everything this chapter is trying to vocalize. Something seems very unsettling about working in a career that you feel doesn't suit you, but you must do it to have a nice life and afford everything you desire. That is not the point of life. As Duchess Meghan says, "It is not enough to just survive something. You've got to thrive! You've got to feel good!"[192] It applies to your career just as much as it applies to your life in my view. Enjoying what you do will add a whole different level of pleasure and quality to your work, which is all you could ever ask for in the field or career. It ensures you will excel. So, try and ask yourself the same question every single day: What do I desire?

---

191 Alexandros Maragos, "Alan Watts: What Do You Desire? (Video)," *Alexandros Maragos* January 5, 2013.

192 *Prince Harry & Duchess Meghan Final Day Royal Tour Africa 2019! Inc Speeches!, YouTube* (YouTube, 2019) accessed July 5, 2020.

Now, I'd like to introduce someone I feel is the perfect example of someone who discovered their passion and ran with it. Lilly Singh is a Girl-Boss who appears to enjoy every part of what her career entails. She always has a smile on her face, she is able to effortlessly make the people around her smile, and she has repeatedly expressed her gratitude for being able to do what she loves and get paid for it. She followed her passion, and it has paid off greatly in her favour. For anyone who is not awaare, Lilly Singh (previously known as iiSuperwomanii) is a professional YouTuber who has gained an immense sense of popularity from making funny videos about her life experiences, her heritage, and comical advice that brightens the day of each of her 14.9 million subscribers.[193] I began watching Lilly's videos when I was around fourteen years old, and I was always left in tears of laughter and joy when her videos finished. She is able to relate to her fans very well. I believe that she was given a gift that is the ability to put a comedic spin on any situation that you encounter, producing an immense amount of happiness. She is unapologetically herself, which is why her unique videos are favoured so highly.

While making people laugh, Lilly has spoken very openly about the struggles within her life and how it led her to discover her passion for making people smile, which she has managed to do through YouTube. In a "Draw My Life" video, Lilly opened up about her struggle with depression and how it led her to one of the lowest points in her life, along with sharing the level of power your mind has in

---

[193] "Lilly Singh," Wikitubia, 2020, accessed July 6, 2020.

controlling you when it comes to negative thoughts.¹⁹⁴ However, through all the darkness, she recognized the power of the mind could be used just as strongly for positivity as it could for negativity, which is where her passion started.¹⁹⁵ From that moment on, Lilly began to chase her passion of making the world smile. She learned how to edit videos and started to put serious effort into her YouTube channel, which was hard to get off the ground but eventually soared high.¹⁹⁶ It has led on to her becoming an author, an actress, and the host of her own talk show, *A Little Late With Lilly Singh*.¹⁹⁷ She is the perfect example of what chasing your passions can lead to. From this view, she is a true Girl-Boss. She is making a positive difference in the world by making all of us smile.

After doing some research, I found another inspiring video that Lilly produced last year on how to find your passion.¹⁹⁸ It was very short, and filled with a lot of insight. She has a special method of phrasing her ideals in such a simple, comprehensible way that leaves a strong impact on you, her audience.¹⁹⁹ The video was memorable, and she shares some personal advice on how pushing her personal boundaries allowed her to find her passion and follow her true calling in life. She explains to the interviewer that she got into a phase

---

194 Deepa Lakshmin, "Exactly 70 People Watched Lilly Singh's First YouTube Video—Now Millions Do," MTV News, October 21, 2015.

195 Ibid.

196 Ibid.

197 "Lilly Singh," Wikitubia, 2020, accessed July 6, 2020.

198 Impact Theory Team, "Lilly Singh," Impact Theory, August 23, 2018.

199 Ibid.

of saying yes to everything. This is what led her to a career with YouTube. She states that: "*A big part of finding out what's right for you is [to] stop confining yourself to a path that you've been convinced is the path.*"[200] This is what she says she is doing now with her career. She is on an unfamiliar career path that was not guaranteed when she first aligned herself with it. She also spoke of this career being very frowned upon within her family: "*For a young Indian girl that's a part of my family, like, this is nowhere on the path. It was very much so 'go to school and get married and have kids and that's a success'. If you're able to have those kids and give [your] mom grandkids, you're successful, and I think it's about really stepping outside of that and exploring [other options of success].*"[201] If we were living in the generation that our parents grew up in, we would never be able to call being a full-time YouTuber a career. But now things have changed, hence, why Lilly is stressing the importance of exploring and opening your eyes to different experiences.

The interviewer went on to ask Lilly how people can be sure they are on the right path while attempting to discover their passions, to which the answer is slightly more simple than you would have imagined. Lilly claims that she just paid attention to what excited her.[202] Some mornings she feels completely sleep deprived (and she *loves* to sleep), but she will still throw herself out of bed due to the excitement she feels about the work day she is about to have. This, and surrounding yourself with the people that support you and love

---

200 Ibid.
201 Ibid.
202 Ibid.

you is very crucial. Lilly believes that supportive people are able to bring out a very beautiful side of you that is creative. It makes you face all of your scenarios in the best way. She also notes that: *"This entire career path has been everything but comfortable, no part of it's comfortable so even on the days when I come home and I think that was horrible . . . I can literally feel part of me evolving as like, OK, what you did and now you know for the next one, what to do, you'll know what to expect for the next one and those scary things are all signs that you're doing [well]."*[203]

Both Lilly's actions and words have shown she has truly practiced what she preaches. She is an incredibly successful woman (as proven by her being the only woman to make it into *Forbes* magazine in 2017) and a fantastic example of a Girl-Boss in the flesh. We can follow in her footsteps and find true passion in our careers in so many ways. It has the benefits of charging your creative powers on a regular basis, not to mention the sense of purpose it gives you. You will make your mark on the world if you live according to your purpose. Life is too short to do something you don't enjoy. Through this endeavour, you are able to achieve authentic happiness. Find the thing that makes you feel invincible and follow that feeling. Keep asking the question Alan Watts was proposing: What do you truly desire? What would you do if money were no object? Don't deny yourself the pleasure. Seek out your passion, and never let it go without a fight.

---

203 Ibid.

Action Points for This Chapter:

- Forget the aspect of money. Find a career in something that excites you to your core.
- Make sure that you have people around you that care for you.
- Don't be afraid to take a different path than the traditional one or you'll never know where it will take you.

ENDING MESSAGE

And that sums it all up!

Here you have it. Your own personal guide to doing your best, according to the masters. Your own little treasure chest of metaphorical jewels to help you smile. I have felt so inspired by every single person I have featured within this book, and I hope you have too.

Being an empowered woman in your own right is something I would only describe as rewarding and liberating. Whether you are advocating for animal rights or protesting about saving our planet, studying for your exams in school or working hard for your money, it all falls under the same Girl-Boss category in my eyes. To establish more familiarity with the information in this book, I chose to include household names that many of you will know. But you do not have to be a well-known A-Lister to be empowering to the women who surround you. Living as the best version of yourself and doing your part to make our world more hospitable is what defines you as empowered/empowering.

Just by reading this book, you have taken the first step in your incredible journey. You should feel proud of yourself, because I do! This is something we are all able to achieve, and the best part of it is that we can all do it together as a sisterhood. Can you imagine the feeling of euphoria you will experience knowing you not only achieved the Girl-Boss status, but you had a hand in ensuring someone else has also?! It is togetherness at its finest, and nothing is better than this!

Although writing this book has been far from easy, I can honestly say that sharing these stories and creating the content has been nothing short of a pleasure. It has truly been worth all the blood, sweat, and tears. It's my first solo project and I am beyond proud of it, simply because I have been able to share it with you all. It makes me smile knowing that I'll be a part of your journey through these words written here. It reminds us that we are all connected.

I cannot thank you enough for taking the time to read this book. Congratulations for getting to the end! Continue to go forth and spread the message! I pray that you will keep this book close to you in times of happiness and sadness. It will be here, available to you whenever you need it. May it always be a source of positivity and provide advice that will bring clarity to you and everyone across the globe.

Sending Love and Light in your direction!

Love Always,

T.H.

APPENDIX

INTRODUCTION

Hawk, Taylor. "Passing on Being Passive: Article." Denison University, November 29, 2016. https://denison.edu/academics/womens-gender-studies/feature/87411.

INGRAHAM, CHRISTOPHER. "Americans Are Becoming Less Happy, and There's Research to Prove It." Los Angeles Times. Los Angeles Times, March 23, 2019. https://www.latimes.com/science/sciencenow/la-sci-sn-americans-less-happy-20190323-story.html.

Morton, Andrew, *Meghan: A Hollywood Princess*, (London, Michael O'Hara Books Ltd, 2018) p. 40-41.

Smith, Roger. "Gender Pay Gap in the UK: 2019." Office for National Statistics. Office for National Statistics, October 29, 2019. https://www.ons.gov.uk/employmentandlabourmarket/peopleinwork/earningsandworkinghours/bulletins/genderpaygapintheuk/2019.

The Queen's Commonwealth Trust, "The Queen's Commonwealth Trust International Women's Day Panel- Full Discussion." March 8, 2019, video, 20:10. https://www.youtube.com/watch?v=6GDsdmouyQg&t=2207s.

CHAPTER 1

"'Chasing Skills, Not Levels,' a Recipe for Women's Success in the Corporate World." The Globe and Mail, September 7, 2019. https://www.theglobeandmail.com/business/adv/article-chasing-skills-not-levels-a-recipe-for-womens-success-in-the/.

"CISD Presents: New Beings and Women's Empowerment Group in Discussion with Baroness Valerie Amos." SOAS Radio, October 31, 2018. https://soasradio.org/tags/valerie-amos.

Baroness Valerie Amos Appointed as Master of University College." University of Oxford, 2019. http://www.ox.ac.uk/news/2019-08-02-baroness-valerie-amos-appointed-master-university-college.

Chappet, Marie-Claire. "Seriously, Why Are We Still Asking If Women Can 'Have It All'?" Glamour. Glamour UK, March 20, 2019. https://www.glamourmagazine.co.uk/article/can-women-have-it-all.

David, Avril. "The 10 Most Powerful Women at the United Nations." Forbes. Forbes Magazine, September 2, 2011. https://www.forbes.com/sites/avrildavid/2011/05/02/the-10-most-powerful-women-at-the-united-nations/.

Duncan, Pamela, and Holder, Josh. "Revealed: Britain's Most Powerful Elite Is 97% White." The Guardian. Guardian News and Media, September 24, 2017. https://www.theguardian.com/inequality/2017/sep/24/revealed-britains-most-powerful-elite-is-97-white.

Paull, Sylvia. "2000: WHAT IS TODAY'S MOST IMPORTANT UNREPORTED STORY?" Edge.org, January 1, 1970. https://www.edge.org/response-detail/11723.

Songfacts. "It's a Man's Man's Man's World by James Brown—Songfacts." Song Meanings at Songfacts. Accessed June 26, 2020. https://www.songfacts.com/facts/james-brown/its-a-mans-mans-mans-world.

The Editors of Encyclopaedia Britannica. "Valerie Ann Amos, Baroness Amos of Brondesbury." Encyclopædia Britannica. Encyclopædia Britannica, inc., March 9, 2020. https://www.britannica.com/biography/Valerie-Ann-Amos-Baroness-Amos-of-Brondesbury.

"Under-Secretary-General for Humanitarian Affairs and Emergency Relief Coordinator, Valerie Amos Statement on Yemen – Yemen." ReliefWeb. Accessed July 5, 2020. https://reliefweb.int/report/yemen/under-secretary-general-humanitarian-affairs-and-emergency-relief-coordinator-valerie.

Ward, Marguerite. "Women Are Afraid to Call Themselves 'Ambitious' at Work and It's Seriously Hurting Their Careers." Business Insider. Business Insider, March 8, 2020.

Watson, Christopher, Elise Uberoi, and Esme Kirk-Wade. "Women in Parliament and Government." House of Commons Library, May 31, 2020. https://commonslibrary.parliament.uk/research-briefings/sn01250/.

Weaver, Matthew. "Valerie Amos and Kofi Annan to Visit Syria—Monday, 5 March 2012." The Guardian. Guardian News and Media, March 5, 2012. https://www.theguardian.com/world/middle-east-live/2012/mar/05/syria-uprising-baba-amr-cleared-live-updates

CHAPTER 2

Achilles, Rebecca. "Oprah Winfrey Credits Her Success to This One Thing We All Have." Medium. Thoughts and Ideas, December 6, 2018. https://medium.com/indian-thoughts/oprah-winfrey-credits-her-success-to-this-one-thing-we-all-have-4435a14b063d.

"Beyoncé—Haunted." Genius, December 13, 2013. https://genius.com/Beyonce-haunted-lyrics.

Buckley, Cara. "Powerful Hollywood Women Unveil Anti-Harassment Action Plan." The New York Times. The New York Times, January 1, 2018. https://www.nytimes.com/2018/01/01/movies/times-up-hollywood-women-sexual-harassment.html.

Candid. "Oprah Winfrey's Angel Network to Dissolve." Philanthropy News Digest (PND), June 1, 2010. https://philanthropynewsdigest.org/news/oprah-winfrey-s-angel-network-to-dissolve.

Crockett, Kathy. "Oprah Winfrey's Leadership Academy for Girls." The MY HERO Project, 2020. https://myhero.com/Oprah_Academy07.

Ferrera, America. "America Ferrera on Activism After the Women's March." Time. Time, March 1, 2018. https://time.com/5171286/america-ferrera-activism-womens-march/.

"George Floyd: 'Pandemic of Racism' Led to His Death, Memorial Told." BBC News. BBC, June 5, 2020. https://www.bbc.co.uk/news/world-us-canada-52928304.

Gillett, Rachel. "How Walt Disney, Oprah Winfrey, and 19 Other Successful People Rebounded After Getting Fired." Inc.com. Inc., October 7, 2015. https://www.inc.com/business-insider/21-successful-people-who-rebounded-after-getting-fired.html.

"Graduating Class of 2019." OWLAG. Accessed July 3, 2020. https://owlag.co.za/.

Howton, Elizabeth. "Nearly Half the World Lives on Less than $5.50 a Day." World Bank, 2018. https://www.worldbank.org/en/news/press-release/2018/10/17/nearly-half-the-world-lives-on-less-than-550-a-day.

Hurst, Katherine. "Cause and Effect Meaning: The 12 Laws of Karma List." The Law of Attraction, October 9, 2019. https://www.thelawofattraction.com/12-laws-karma/.

Moer, Christian. "Child Mortality Rate Drops by a Third since 1990." UNICEF, September 16, 2010. https://www.unicef.org/media/media_56045.html.

Ogbogu, Stephanie. "Oprah Is the Richest Black Woman in the World." AfroTech, 2020. https://afrotech.com/oprah-richest-black-woman.

"Overview." World Bank, 2020. https://www.worldbank.org/en/topic/poverty/overview.

"Rhonda Byrne Biography: The Secret—Official Website." The Official Website of The Secret. Accessed July 3, 2020. https://www.thesecret.tv/about/rhonda-byrnes-biography/.

Spear's, July 6, 2020 by "Oprah Winfrey's Net Worth." Spear's Magazine, January 25, 2018. https://www.spearswms.com/oprah-winfrey-net-worth/.

CHAPTER 3

Borge, Jonathan. "America Ferrera Explains the Importance of the Time's Up Initiative." InStyle, 2018. https://www.instyle.com/news/america-ferrera-times-up-today-show-interview.

Ferrera, America. "My Identity Is a Superpower—Not an Obstacle." TED, 2019. https://www.ted.com/talks/america_ferrera_my_identity_is_a_superpower_not_an_obstacle?language=en.

McLaughlin, Posted by Denis. "Leaders: All the World's a Stage. And All the Men and Women Are Merely Players." denisgmclaughlin.com, September 16, 2013. https://denisgmclaughlin.

com/leaders-all-the-worlds-a-stage-and-all-the-men-and-women-are-merely-players/.

Radford, Jynnah. "Key Findings about U.S. Immigrants." Pew Research Center. Pew Research Center, June 17, 2019. https://www.pewresearch.org/fact-tank/2019/06/17/key-findings-about-u-s-immigrants/.

Rodriguez, Mathew. "America Ferrera's Women's March Address Stood in Solidarity with Young Undocumented Immigrants." Mic. Mic, January 21, 2017. https://www.mic.com/articles/166240/america-ferreras-womens-march-address-stood-in-solidarity-with-young-undocumented-immigrants.

McAfee, Tierney. "America Ferrera at D.C. Women's March: 'The President Is Not America. . . . We Are America.'" EW.com, 2017. https://ew.com/news/2017/01/21/america-ferrera-dc-womens-march/.

CHAPTER 4

"How to Stop Negative Self-Talk." Mayo Clinic. Mayo Foundation for Medical Education and Research, January 21, 2020. https://www.mayoclinic.org/healthy-lifestyle/stress-management/in-depth/positive-thinking/art-20043950.

Himmelman, Peter. "The Power of Positive Speech: How Choosing the Right Words Defines Your Reality." Forbes. Forbes Magazine, October 23, 2018. https://www.forbes.com/sites/peterhimmelman/2018/10/21/the-power-of-positive-speech-how-choosing-the-right-words-defines-your-reality/.

Howes, Lewis. "Cultivate an Attitude of Gratitude." April 30, 2020. https://lewishowes.com/podcast/attitude-of-gratitude/.

TedXTalks. "The Power of Gratitude and Positive Thinking," Dareen Nasr- TedX AlRabihSchool, July 19, 2019, 9:52 minutes. https://www.youtube.com/watch?v=akeJenIyaEc.

CHAPTER 5:

National Association of Anorexia Nervosa and Associated Disorders. "Eating Disorders Statistics." ANAD. Accessed February 24, 2014, http://www.anad.org/get-information/about-eating-disorders/eating-disorders-statistics/.

Young&BosSHE. "About." Content and Resources for SHEs, by SHEs, November 10, 2019. http://youngbosshe.org/about/.

CHAPTER 6:

Burchard, Brendon. "How to Bring the Joy to Every Situation." Brendon Burchard, July 27, 2016. https://brendon.com/blog/bringthejoy/.

Do It Well. Make It Fun: The Key to Finding Balance during Times of Stress, Adulthood, & Death. Place of publication not identified, Texas: Greenleaf Book Group LLC, 2012.

Updated November 24, Gonzalez, Sandra. "Modern Family Recap: Season 3, Episode 9: Punkin Chunkin." EW.com, 2011. https://ew.com/recap/modern-family-recap-punkin-chunkin/.

"Responsibility and Response: Why Our Choices Are the Only Thing That Matters." Daily Stoic, November 25, 2017. https://dailystoic.com/responsibility-and-response/.

Sanchez, Chelsey. "Meghan Markle on Royal Life: 'It's Not Enough to Just Survive.'" Harper's BAZAAR. Harper's BAZAAR, October 21, 2019. https://www.harpersbazaar.com/celebrity/latest/a29534886/meghan-markle-survive-thrive-quote/.

Schawbel, Dan. "Why You Need to Have Fun to Be Successful." Forbes. Forbes Magazine, September 20, 2013. https://www.forbes.com/sites/danschawbel/2012/07/25/why-you-need-to-have-fun-to-be-successful/.

Warburton, Nigel. *Little History of Philosophy* (New Haven, Connecticut: Yale University Press, 2014), accessed on July 5, 2020.

CHAPTER 7:

Brockes, Emma. "#MeToo Founder Tarana Burke: 'You Have to Use Your Privilege to Serve Other People.'" The Guardian. Guardian News and Media, January 15, 2018. https://www.theguardian.com/world/2018/jan/15/me-too-founder-tarana-burke-women-sexual-assault.

Dockterman, Eliana. "One Reason Why Oscars Shut Women Out of Best Director." Time. Time, January 13, 2020. https://time.com/5763937/oscars-2020-female-directors-shut-out/.

Girish, Devika. "'On the Record' Review: A Black Woman Says '#MeToo.'" The New York Times. The New York Times, May 27,

2020. https://www.nytimes.com/2020/05/27/movies/on-the-record-russell-simmons-review.html.

Harvey Weinstein Timeline: How the Scandal Unfolded." BBC News. BBC, May 29, 2020. https://www.bbc.co.uk/news/entertainment-arts-41594672.

Kavanagh, Joanne. "We Reveal All about #MeToo and the Most Recent Sex Abuse Allegations." The Sun. The Sun, April 18, 2018. https://www.thesun.co.uk/tvandshowbiz/4700676/me-too-metoo-harvey-weinstein-donald-trump/.

Nicolaou, Elena. "Ashley Judd Was a #MeToo Heroine Years Before the Movement Began: A Timeline." Timeline of Ashley Judd's Participation In #MeToo, #TimesUp, 2018. https://www.refinery29.com/en-gb/2018/05/198128/ashley-judd-weinstein-lawsuit-timeline-metoo-movement.

Times Up UK. "TIME'S UP UK Is an Organisation That Insists on Safe, Fair and Dignified Work for Everyone." Times Up UK, October 2, 1970. https://www.timesupuk.org/news/celebrating-female-representation-at-this-year-bfi-london-film-festival/.

CHAPTER 8

Anand, Shafali R. "Courage Is the First Virtue—Knowledge Is the Second!" The Zen of Learning, February 3, 2010. https://thezenoflearning.wordpress.com/2010/02/03/courage-knowledge-learning-aristotle/.

Breaking News, Dr. Brené Brown is on SuperSoul today talking about transcending failure and RISING STRONG, November 12, 2017, video, 43m27s, https://www.youtube.com/watch?v=D-FaA7mvgMNk.

Bridges, Frances. "5 Ways to Be Brave According to Brené Brown's Netflix Special 'The Call to Courage.'" Forbes. Forbes Magazine, April 30, 2019. https://www.forbes.com/sites/francesbridges/2019/04/29/5-ways-to-be-brave-according-to-brene-browns-netflix-special-the-call-to-courage/.

Brown, Brené, Daring Greatly: How the Courage to Be Vulnerable Transforms the Way We Live, Love, Parent, and Lead. New York: Avery, 2012.

Brown, Brené. "About." Brené Brown, 2020. https://brenebrown.com/about/.

Brown, Brené. "Dr. Brené Brown Archives." SuperSoul.tv. Accessed July 7, 2020. http://www.supersoul.tv/tag/dr-brene-brown.

Brown, Brené. "The Power of Vulnerability." TED, 2020. https://www.ted.com/talks/brene_brown_the_power_of_vulnerability.

Chapman, Gary, Lysa TerKeurst, Glennon Doyle Melton, Brené Brown, Mindy Kaling, Aziz Ansari with Eric Klinenberg, Wednesday Martin, Jennifer Weiner, A. E. Hotchner, and Helen Macdonald. "Love and Relationships Books: Best Sellers, Dec. 11, 2016." The New York Times. The New York Times, 2016. https://www.nytimes.com/books/best-sellers/2016/12/11/relationships/.

Vincent, Alice. "'I Wrote It in Four Hours': The Woman Responsible for the Wisdom of Baz Luhrmann's Everybody's Free to Wear Sunscreen, 20 Years On." The Telegraph. Telegraph Media Group, May 29, 2017. https://www.telegraph.co.uk/music/artists/wrote-four-hours-woman-responsible-wisdom-baz-luhrmanns-wear/.

CHAPTER 9:

"Emma Grede: Women for Women International." TWICE the impact for women survivors of war. Accessed July 3, 2020. https://www.womenforwomen.org/about/our-team/emma-grede.

Gross, Elana Lyn. "How Emma Grede And Khloe Kardashian Are Building Their Size-Inclusive Fashion Line Good American." Forbes. Forbes Magazine, June 3, 2019. https://www.forbes.com/sites/elanagross/2019/05/28/good-american/.

Keeping up with the Kardashians, 'Kim's Last Ditch Effort,' PrimeVideo, 43m45s, April 2, 2017, https://www.amazon.co.uk/gp/video/detail/B06XJK6KSV/ref=atv_dp_season_select_s13.

Lodeiro, Fernanda. "The Secret Spot Where I Found Love: A Lesson in the Law of Detachment." HuffPost. HuffPost, February 9, 2015. https://www.huffpost.com/entry/the-secret-spot-where-i-found-love_b_6294792.

Nurick, Jen. "Khloe Kardashian's Good American Denim Line Made USD$1 Million in Its First Day." Vogue Australia, January 16, 2018. https://www.vogue.com.au/fashion/news/khloe-kardashians-good-american-denim-line-made-usd1-million-in-its-first-day/news-story/3b7264899016de1a1adadc6bf6e8aab9.

"Our Story." Women for Women International. Accessed July 3, 2020. https://www.womenforwomen.org.uk/about-us/our-story.

WomenForWomenUK, "Brita Fernandez-Schmidt and Emma Grede discuss the power of feminism in Facebook Live Chat" May 21, 2018, video, 26m24s, https://www.youtube.com/watch?v=l2RfgX2LrsQ.

CHAPTER 10:

Curie, Marie. "Marie Curie the Scientist: Biog, Facts & Quotes." Marie Curie, 2020. https://www.mariecurie.org.uk/who/our-history/marie-curie-the-scientist.

History.com. "Hillary Clinton Is Elected to the U.S. Senate." History.com. A&E Television Networks, July 24, 2019. https://www.history.com/this-day-in-history/hillary-clinton-elected-to-senate-new-york.

Leight, Elias. "Koffee Makes History with Grammy Win, Signs with RCA." Rolling Stone. Rolling Stone, February 7, 2020. https://www.rollingstone.com/music/music-features/koffee-grammy-win-rca-signing-946992/.

Leslie, S. "Koffee Youngest Reggae/Dancehall Artist to Top Billboard Chart." Urban Islandz, April 1, 2019. https://urbanislandz.com/2019/04/01/koffee-reggae-dancehall-sensation-tops-billboard-chart/.

"Maya Angelou." Academy of Achievement, November 7, 2019. https://achievement.org/achiever/maya-angelou/.

"Michelle Obama Popularity Polls—Washington Post." The Washington Post. WP Company, 2016. https://www.washingtonpost.com/gdpr-consent/?next_url=https%3A%2F%2Fwww.washingtonpost.com%2Fgraphics%2Fnational%2Fobama-legacy%2Fmichelle-obama-popularity.html.

Music, Apple. "Koffee on Apple Music." Apple Music, 2020. https://music.apple.com/gb/artist/koffee/188842448.

Reggaeville. "Biography: Koffee." www.reggaeville.com. Accessed July 3, 2020. https://www.reggaeville.com/artist-details/koffee/about/.

CHAPTER 11:

Maragos, Alexandros. "Alan Watts: What Do You Desire? (Video)." January 5, 2013. https://alexandrosmaragos.com/blog/2013/01/alan-watts.

Markle, Meghan. "The Girl Power Speech That Put Meghan Markle on the Map." The Sydney Morning Herald. The Sydney Morning Herald, October 9, 2018. https://www.smh.com.au/lifestyle/life-and-relationships/the-girl-power-speech-that-put-meghan-markle-on-the-map-20181009-p508lb.html.

Prince Harry & Duchess Meghan Final Day Royal Tour Africa 2019! Inc Speeches! YouTube. YouTube, 2019. https://www.youtube.com/watch?v=M9zxGZ4AMfE.

CHAPTER 12:

Dray, Kayleigh. "Caroline Flack Inspired Us to Be Kind. Why Can't We Do That with Meghan?" Stylist. Stylist, February 29, 2020. https://www.stylist.co.uk/people/meghan-markle-villain-blamed-prince-harry-leaving-monarchy-upsetting-queen-royal-family/361416.

Gordon, Bryony. "Behind the Scenes with Meghan Markle: Duchess Tells Bryony Gordon How Vulnerability Is One of Humanity's Greatest Strengths." The Telegraph. Telegraph Media Group, October 31, 2019. https://www.telegraph.co.uk/royal-family/2019/10/31/behind-scenes-meghan-markle-duchess-tells-bryony-gordon-vulnerability/.

Lakshmin, Deepa. "Exactly 70 People Watched Lilly Singh's First YouTube Video—Now Millions Do." MTV News, October 21, 2015. http://www.mtv.com/news/2342360/lilly-singh-iisuperwomanii-youtube-interview/.

Markle, Meghan. "The Girl Power Speech That Put Meghan Markle on the Map." The Sydney Morning Herald. The Sydney Morning Herald, October 9, 2018. https://www.smh.com.au/lifestyle/life-and-relationships/the-girl-power-speech-that-put-meghan-markle-on-the-map-20181009-p508lb.html.

McLaren, Bonnie. "ITV's Tom Bradby Explains How He Found A 'Bruised and Vulnerable' Prince Harry and Meghan Markle." Grazia. Grazia, October 24, 2019. https://graziadaily.co.uk/celebrity/news/prince-harry-meghan-markle-tom-bradby/.

Regina, The Right Side of History, Twitter post, February 9, 2020, accessed on July 6, 2020. https://twitter.com/regina74/status/1226458735209582592

The Queen's Commonwealth Trust, 2020. https://www.queenscommonwealthtrust.org/.

Wynne, Amelia. "#WeLoveYouMeghan: Outpouring of Support for Duchess of Sussex." Daily Mail Online. Associated Newspapers, October 20, 2019. https://www.dailymail.co.uk/news/article-7591963/WeLoveYouMeghan-Outpouring-support-Duchess-Sussex.html.

www.ingramcontent.com/pod-product-compliance
Lightning Source LLC
LaVergne TN
LVHW011838060526
838200LV00054B/4084